Thank you for your friendship
over the years.
Wishing you and the sisters a
fulfilling ministry in Grange.
With our love & best regards,
Margaret & Peter

A Sheltering Tree

A
SHELTERING
TREE

Inspirational Stories of Faith,
Fidelity, and Friendship

Peter C. Wilcox, STD

WIPF & STOCK · Eugene, Oregon

Wipf & Stock
An Imprint of Wipf and Stock Publishers
199 W. 8th Ave., Suite 3
Eugene, OR 97401

www.wipfandstock.com

ISBN 13: 978–1–62564–665–1

Manufactured in the U.S.A.

For all the friends who have been "special graces" to me on my journey through life. Especially for my wife, Margaret, my best friend, for her love, support, and encouragement and for my daughter, Colleen, whose youthfulness and spontaneity has kept me young. You have all been "bright mirrors of the steadfast, overflowing reality of God's eternal love."

Contents

Preface

Several times a week I receive e-mails from Facebook inviting me to "befriend" someone. Sometimes these invitations come from people whose names I recognize—new neighbors, former students, people whom I have recently met, and the like. At other times, I am puzzled by the invitation; even after reading the person's profile, I can't recall meeting the person or discover any plausible connection. Since I have a very common name, I find myself wondering whether the Facebook invitation was sent by mistake to the wrong person or whether I am just a potential number on that person's list of "friends"—some people seem prone to measure friends by quantity rather than quality.

If you are really interested in "quality-friendships"—then this is definitely a book for you. Yet, I must add a few words of caution. First *caveat*: this book is not bed-time reading. Not long ago, I read a book on medieval theology—it was a great sleep-inducer! After half a dozen pages or so, I was ready for bed. In contrast, I found this book by Peter Wilcox hard to put down. After reading a story or a lesson, I was often tempted to read "just one more." So, if this book keeps you awake or—better—wakes up some buried thoughts about your friendships, past and present, don't say you weren't forewarned.

Second *caveat*: since this book is about the quality of friendships, you may start to feel uneasy—especially if you haven't been the most dependable of friends. Yet instead of feeling guilty, you may soon find yourself motivated to get together with friends whom you haven't seen for some time. So you're alerted in advance that this book may prompt you to revitalize old friendships or establish new friendships—an endeavor that should turn out to be an extraordinarily enjoyable way to spend your free time.

Third *caveat*: if you start thinking about the quality of your friendships, you may realize that some of your friendships have come to include some bad habits or unhealthy pursuits. This book emphasizes that quality friendships should really bring out the best in our friends and us. So you are advised in advance that this book may help you and your friends to abandon detrimental activities and adopt a more healthy and wholesome life-style.

Fourth *caveat*: since a basic premise of this book is that the quality of our friendships with other people is often an indicator of our friendship with God, this book may alert you to the fact that a person has—consciously or unconsciously—been trying to lead a "God-less" life. So you are cautioned in advance that when anyone really tries to improve the quality of her or his friendships, they may find themselves drawing closer to God in love.

In sum, this book is an enjoyable "read"—yet like all self-improvement books, it is not merely a book to be read for entertainment, but a set of lessons to be implemented in life for a better life: you may find yourself wanting to draw closer both to God and to your friends. Presumably that would be appreciated by both your friends and God.

—John T. Ford, C. S. C.

Introduction

Everybody is a story. Every person has a story. When I was a child growing up in West Virginia, my relatives would sit around a large dining room table telling their stories. We don't do that very much anymore. But telling stories is not just a way of passing time. It is the way wisdom gets passed along, the stuff that helps us live a life worth remembering. Despite the awesome powers of technology, many of us still do not live very well. We may need to listen to each other's stories once again.

My grandparents and some other relatives were immigrants from Italy. Gathered around that dining room table, the adults would often share stories of their childhoods in Italy, their coming to America, and the many hardships they had to endure. As children, we would listen intently to what they said, fascinated by their experiences. It is amazing how those times drew our family closer together and taught us so many things about life. I now call it wisdom. Stories are one of the ways life teaches us how to live.

When we don't have the time to listen to each other's stories, we seek out experts to tell us how to live. The less time we spend together at the dining room table, the more how-to books appear in the stores and on our bookshelves. But reading such books is a very different thing than listening to someone's lived experience. Because we have stopped listening to each other, we may even have forgotten how to listen. We have become solitary—readers and watchers rather than sharers and participants.

I have been a theologian and psychotherapist for over thirty years. I spent much of that time learning how to fix life as a psychotherapist, only to discover at the end of the day that life is not broken. It is a mystery to be lived. As Rainer Maria Rilke says, "be patient toward all that is unsolved in your heart, and try to love the questions themselves."[1] Although this approach to life is challenging, it is also more freeing. Realizing we don't have to fix everyone and every situation gives us more opportunities to reflect on the important questions life has to offer and to realize there are no easy or simple answers to many of these questions.

I often asked my clients to tell me their story. It was interesting because so often they would tell me about their achievements or what they had acquired or built over a lifetime. So many of us do not know our own story: about who we are, not what we have done; about what we have felt, thought, feared and discovered through the events of our lives.

Stories are one's *experience* of the events of their life; they are not the events themselves. When shared with us, stories allow us to see something familiar through new eyes. We become in that moment a guest in another's life, and together with them sit at the feet of their teacher. If we think we have no stories, it is because we have not paid enough attention to our lives. Most of us live lives that are far richer and more meaningful than we appreciate.

It is very interesting in life to see how we can remember certain things long after they occur. Back in the 1970s, I was working on my doctorate in theology at Catholic University. In one of my classes my professor, who was sharing some stories about relationships, made a statement that I have never forgotten. "If you have a relationship in life that is good, there is hardly anything better; if you have one that is bad, there is hardly anything worse."

This book is about stories of faith, fidelity, and friendship. Utilizing both Christian and non-Christian writers, it explores their ideas about friendship and investigates how friendships have been important in their psychological and spiritual development. From a Christian perspective, it looks at the importance of friends,

1. Rilke, *Letters to a Young Poet*, 35.

even for saints. Often, when we read about the saints, we don't usually focus on the role of friends in their lives. But for many of them, friends were an important part of their spiritual lives. Their teachings on friendship can be very helpful to us in our own growth and development. Finally, this book explores fifteen lessons about friendship for our own times with some contemporary stories. These stories of faith, fidelity, and friendship can be sources of encouragement and inspiration for each of us on our journeys, leading us closer to each other and to the Lord who has called each of us his friend.

1

Two Graced Moments

CARYLL HOUSELANDER: "UNDERGROUND TRAIN VISION"

In 1955 Caryll Houselander described an experience of grace that had a profound impact on her life:

> I was in an underground train, a crowded train in which all sorts of people jostled together, sitting and strap-hanging—workers of every description going home at the end of the day. Quite suddenly I saw with my mind, but as vividly as a wonderful picture, Christ in them all. But I saw more than that, not only was Christ in every one of them, living in them, dying in them, rejoicing in them—but because he was in them, and because they were here, the whole world was here too, here in this underground train; not only the world as it was at that moment, not only all the people in all the countries of the world, but all those people who had lived in the past, and all those yet to come. . . . I came out into the street and walked for a long time in the crowds. It was the same here, on every side, in every passer-by, everywhere—Christ.[1]

1. Houselander, *A Rocking Horse Catholic*, 137–38; see http://www.archive.

Later on, sometime around the end of World War II, author and publisher Maisie Ward had an appointment to meet Caryll. Until this time she had only known her through correspondence and her published works. With her husband Frank Sheed, she had, in fact, been responsible for the publication of some of those works. However, unlike him, she had never been in the author's presence. The first meeting between Maisie Ward and Caryll Houselander is both intriguing and poignant. She recorded it some years after it happened in the biography Maisie wrote about her friend:

> It is always interesting to meet for the first time someone known intimately by correspondence. My husband had prepared me for Caryll's appearance—as it had seemed to me in an exaggerated fashion. Yet as I stood waiting outside the door of her flat and she came up behind me laden with parcels, I was conscious of a genuine shock. The dead white face, the thick glasses, the fringe of red hair, a touch somehow of the grotesque—it was so surprising as to take one's breath away. But we had hardly exchanged a word when we felt (both of us, I could swear) the perfect ease of long intimacy, and began a conversation to be picked up at any moment thereafter. It was not until much later that I found she had used the word grotesque about herself.[2]

Grotesque or not, Maisie Ward had met a remarkable woman whose entire life was animated by her profound sense of the presence of Christ in everyone. While she had the particular grace of receiving this understanding in her "underground train vision," Caryll struggled at times to keep that realization alive, often able to do so only through what she called "a deliberate and blind act of faith."[3] Her success at holding fast to her conviction of Christ's abiding presence is evident in her spiritual writings and in the work she did with the psychologically wounded of all ages, whom,

---

org/details/rockinghorsecath008000mbp.

2. Ward, *Caryll Houselander*, 206.

3. Houselander, *A Rocking Horse Catholic*, 140.

as one doctor put it, "she loved . . . back to life."[4] She herself wrote at the end of her autobiography: "The realization of our oneness in Christ is the only cure for human loneliness. For me, too, it is the only ultimate meaning of life, the only thing that gives meaning and purpose to every life."[5]

Despite her outward eccentricity, Caryll Houselander was a docile and willing instrument in the hands of God. She was one of those "weak" and "foolish" things (1 Cor. 1:27)[6] that God delights in using in a variety of ways. Motivated by the certainty of Christ alive in her and everyone else and acutely aware of the touch of God's grace in her own life, Caryll was an open channel for the outpouring of that grace to others. She was a true friend. Maisie Ward remembered the easy intimacy she felt with Caryll on her first meeting. Both her devoted circle of friends and the many others to whom she ministered were enduring testimonies of her faithfulness to the great commandments of loving God and one another. She knew that human life was the arena where God made himself known, even to the point of becoming one with us. Maisie Ward called the task of discovering God in ourselves and in all those we meet "the main testing of the Christian life," and her friend Caryll understood this significance of that test very well.

THOMAS MERTON: "FOURTH AND WALNUT EXPERIENCE"

Three years later, in March 1958, Thomas Merton had an experience that profoundly changed his attitude toward people and the world, allowing him to "occupy himself critically" with it.[7] He was walking through the shopping district of downtown Louisville when, in the middle of a crowd of people, he had a vision that he later recorded in his journal:

4. Ward, *Caryll Houselander*, 263.

5. Houselander, *A Rocking Horse Catholic*, 140.

6. Unless otherwise noted, Scripture quotations are from the New American Bible, available at www.usccb.org/bible.

7. Nouwen, *Pray to Live*, 41.

> In Louisville, at the corner of Fourth and Walnut, in the center of the shopping district, I was suddenly overwhelmed with the realization that I loved all these people, that they were mine and I theirs, that we could not be alien to one another even though we were total strangers. It was like waking from a dream of separateness, of spurious self-isolation in a special world, the world of renunciation and supposed holiness. . . . It was as if I suddenly saw the secret beauty of their hearts, the depths of their hearts where neither sin nor desire nor self-knowledge can reach, the core of their reality, the person that each one is in God's eyes. If only they could all see themselves as they really are. If only we could see each other that way all the time. There would be no more war, no more hatred, no more cruelty, no more greed. . . . I suppose the big problem would be that we would fall down and worship each other.[8]

The world Merton returned to was a world transfigured by his contemplative vision. It was a world he now saw through the eyes of compassion. This new and profound sense of compassion led Merton to take a second look at people and the world, and, interestingly enough, what he saw was not very different from what he himself had experienced in his seventeen years as a Trappist monk. What Merton saw was a world of human beings, vulnerable, confused, desperate, hopeful, just as he was. Reflecting on this experience, Henri Nouwen wrote, "Merton knew . . . that the sin, evil and violence that he found in the world, were the same sin, the same evil, and the same violence that he had discovered in his own heart through solitude, silence and prayer. The impurity in the world was a mirror of the impurity in his own heart."[9] It was only when Merton had found the image of God within himself—his true self--that he could then begin to truly and unselfishly love others.

Merton had come to discover that true solitude enabled him to find his authentic self and others as his brothers and sisters. In

8. Merton, *Conjectures of a Guilty Bystander*, 156–57.
9. Nouwen, *Pray to Live*, 63.

this sense, true solitude for Merton, became all inclusive. It never closes its mind or heart but continually expands in love and compassion towards others. It is through true solitude that Merton found healing, because in this solitude he experienced the love of God. In *Disputed Questions*, Merton writes: "This solitary . . . seeks a spiritual and simple oneness in himself which, when it is found, paradoxically becomes the oneness of all men."[10] Merton believed if each person could find his own solitude, especially amidst the confusion of daily life, only then would a healthy, love-filled society result. He came to join solitude with love, showing the true unity of the solitary life is the one in which there is no possible division. The true solitary does not seek himself but loses himself. Therefore, for Merton, when we become one with our true self we become one with all.

William Shannon notes the irony that this mystical experience took place, not in the monastery chapel or in the monastery's woods, but in the very center of a shopping district. It was when other human beings surrounded him that he had the most life-altering, mystical encounter. These were the same human beings who Merton had attempted to hide from when he entered Gethsemani. Shannon comments: "Little did Merton realize when he spoke his exuberant farewell to the world that his interior journey would bring him back once again into the world he thought he had forsaken."[11] Unknown to Merton, it was his own monastic vocation that would eventually come full circle and lead him back into the very same world he had left behind seventeen years earlier.

From this point onward, Merton's life took a drastic turn toward the world and other people. Friendship became much more important to him. He increased his correspondence to his friends and close associates and began to write more to authors, poets, social activists, Sufis, rabbis, Zen masters and theologians among others. Merton wrote to Dorothy Day in support of her Catholic Worker movement, and to simply let her know she was in his prayers. He wrote to psychoanalyst Erich Fromm about his works

10. Merton, *Disputed Questions*, 168.
11. Shannon, *Silent Lamp*, 178.

on the de-humanization of society. He wrote to Abraham Heschel about the nature of prophecy. He wrote to D. T. Suzuki about the Zen Koan tradition, among many other subjects. He wrote to Pope John XXIII after his election and Jacqueline Kennedy and Coretta Scott King after their husbands were assassinated. One common theme characteristic of all Merton's correspondence, however, was its warmth and sincerity. Merton wanted nothing more than to learn about, share with, and show love to these people.

Merton's Fourth and Walnut experience proved to him that contemplation is intimately related to social concern and other people. He came to understand that contemplation is a journey into the desert of our own soul in order to discover there the meaning and mystery of life. He believed the self is always intimately related to the other by compassion. He came to learn that "we do not go into the desert to escape people but to learn how to find them; we do not leave them in order to have nothing more to do with them, but to find out the way to do them the most good."[12] It was only in this way that he could be a genuine friend to others.

12. Merton, *New Seeds of Contemplation*, 80.

2

An Ache in Our Soul

AN INNER RESTLESSNESS

There can be no doubt that we live in an age of revolutionary change and enormous potential. Advances in medical research and pharmacology continually broaden the range of available therapies for many illnesses. Greater understanding of human physiology and nutrition has helped to raise the consciousness of the general public regarding issues of personal health. In the field of information technology, the astoundingly rapid development of computers, smart phones, and social media has made communication instantly available to almost everyone. Many Americans have a higher standard of living than ever and can afford the attractive things a rich economy offers. We are also a highly mobile people, able and willing to go wherever the most promising opportunities beckon.

Despite these recent cultural advances, there are also many implications for how we see ourselves and other people. The atmosphere of rapid, unending change in which people live causes them in Michael Downey's assessment, "to feel that they have been cut loose from those past securities which provided them with a sense of meaning, purpose and value."[1] Advances in genetic engineering, to cite a prominent example, present possibilities for better food production and future cures for illnesses, but they are also creating difficult philosophical, ethical, political, and theological questions. The new world of the internet gives instant information but often eliminates the need to interact with other people. The dazzling array of consumer choices is a tribute to a very healthy economy, but it also encourages an aggressive advertising industry to create its own standards of what people should need, desire, and value. Reflecting on the effects of this heightened consumerism, Wilkie Au wrote: "Inner voices disturb our peace and tell us that we are not good-looking enough, not smart enough, not rich enough, not talented enough. Advertisements displaying societally acclaimed examples of successful and beautiful people either create or reinforce our inner doubts."[2]

This resulting inner restlessness contributes to the rootlessness so characteristic of modern society. It becomes more difficult to make the kinds of connections that could be lasting. Many of us are only superficially able to know the "joys and constraints that come from being part of a set community with consistent relationships."[3] We continually try to become more self-sufficient, shaping our own futures. Independence rather than interdependence becomes primary, and, in Michael Downey's words, "we are individuals before we are community . . . we are selves prior to being in communion with others."[4]

LONGING FOR INTEGRATION

Although many possess a certain fundamental dissatisfaction, we also know there is a need for a "center" that a technologically oriented, increasingly impersonal culture cannot provide. "There is

1. Downey, *Understanding Christian Spirituality*, 17.
2. Au, *By Way of the Heart*, 27–28.
3. Crossin, *Friendship*, 6.
4. Downey, *Understanding Christian Spirituality*, 18.

an ache in the soul, a longing for more than meets the eye."[5] Avery Dulles described that ache in this way: "In their hearts, people long for something more than is offered by the secular order, with its passing pleasures and fluctuating opinions. They reach out for something higher, something universally and eternally good and true, to which they can give themselves permanently and totally."[6]

This ache for "something more" is a search for a way to integrate the competing demands of everyday life. We yearn to be whole, we long for integration. We seek to give coherent expression to a vital energy within us that is reflective of our deepest desires for meaning. Ronald Rolheiser calls this longing "a congenital all-embracing ache that lies at the center of human experience and is the ultimate force that drives everything else."[7]

This longing, this "ache within our soul," drives us out of ourselves toward God and other people to seek fulfillment. Scott Peck points out that "we can never be completely whole in and of ourselves. . . . It is true that we are created to be individually unique. Yet the reality is that we are inevitably social creatures who desperately need each other not merely for sustenance, not merely for company, but for any meaning in our lives whatsoever."[8]

The fullness of our own accomplishments and the strength of our independence will not serve to meet this fundamental ache within. Our acquisitions cannot address it. This is because the deepest sentiments of the human heart draw us out of ourselves, not to a place of status, but to interconnection—to a recognition of our identity as inevitably social creatures that desperately need each other. Neither the pressures nor the attractions of a world moving at lightning speed are to divert us from seeking "the first and most necessary gift . . . love."[9] In the challenge of our contemporary milieu, this "most necessary gift" is the graceful energy that enables us to answer the call to holiness. It is this "touch of the di-

---

5. Ibid., 6.
6. Dulles, "Orthodoxy and Social Change," 14.
7. Rolheiser, *The Holy Longing*, 4.
8. Peck, *The Different Drum*, 54–55.
9. Second Vatican Council, *Dogmatic Constitution on the Church*, 42.

vine within us" that Caryll Houselander and Thomas Merton came to understand in their "graced moments"—that Christ is present within each of us, "that we could not be alien to one another even though we were total strangers." It was in this realization that we are all called to find fulfillment in our connectedness to one another.

3

The Grace of Friendship

AN UNQUENCHABLE FIRE

There is within every one of us, Alan Jones wrote, "a terrific thing."[1]
Ronald Rolheiser called it "an unquenchable fire . . . a longing . . .
a wildness that cannot be tamed."[2] It does not depend at all on attractiveness, status, accomplishments, intelligence, or capability. It
is not defined through how much we can achieve or how efficient
we are in handling the various dimensions of our lives. Rather, it is
part of the very essence of who we are, and, as a powerful energy,
it fuels the fundamental yearning we have for meaning, for something beyond just ourselves. Gerald May identified this "terrific
thing," this unquenchable fire in all of us as our desire "to love, to
be loved, to know love," and "our true identity, our reason for being, is to be found in this desire."[3] This is our deepest call, the seat
of our deepest desires, and the most authentic statement of who

---

1. Jones, *Exploring Spiritual Direction*, 42.
2. Rolheiser, *The Holy Longing*, 4.
3. May, *The Awakened Heart*, 1.

we are meant to be. "We are created by love, to live in love, for the sake of love."[4]

As we learn to recognize this energy of love within us individually, we also, like Caryll Houselander and Thomas Merton, come to a more profound appreciation of its existence in everyone else. The differences in us—whether of age, gender, socio-economic status, race, national origin, religion, intelligence, or achievement—are varied expressions of the same simple truth. Comparing us to a human symphony, Gerald May put it beautifully: "They are the tones, instruments, cadences, and chords of the human symphony, arising fresh in each moment, sounding through time. The sound may seem harmonious or discordant, sweet or harsh, but it is one song of love."[5]

We are, in the most fundamental way, linked to each other. This is what Caryll Houselander and Thomas Merton profoundly understood after their graced experiences. This deep and ever-present yearning of love within us calls each of us to recognize that connection and to respond to it. Despite our individual circumstances and quite independent of anything we may accomplish, we are bound to each other through an invisible chord of grace. In the multiplicity of roles each of us has, there is a common one we share with every other person: to be in ourselves visible signs of the grace, which is love, and to see in others the presence of that same grace. We are created for each other and we are created like each other, companions in a common desire to give expression to our truest selves.

CLOTHED WITH RESPECT

Psychiatrist, teacher, and author Robert Coles has written a moving account of the day in 1952 when, as a young and discouraged medical student, he met Dorothy Day. He found himself one afternoon at the Catholic Worker soup kitchen, having made an earlier

4. Ibid., 16.
5. Ibid., 17.

decision to engage in some useful volunteer work. This is the story
of his first encounter with Dorothy:

> She was sitting at a table, talking with a woman who was,
> I quickly realized, quite drunk, yet determined to carry
> on a conversation. . . . The woman to whom Dorothy
> Day was talking . . . had a large purple birthmark along
> the right side of her forehead. She kept touching it as she
> uttered one exclamatory remark after another, none of
> which seemed to get the slightest rise from the person
> sitting opposite her.
>
> I found myself increasingly confused by what seemed
> to be an interminable essentially absurd exchange taking
> place between two middle-aged women. When would
> it end—the alcoholic ranting and the silent nodding,
> occasionally interrupted by a brief question, which
> only served, maddeningly, to wind up the already over-
> talkative one rather than wind her down? Finally, silence
> fell upon the room. She got up and came over to me. She
> said, "Are you waiting to talk to one of us?"
>
> *One of us*: with those three words she had cut through
> layers of self-importance, a life-time of bourgeois privi-
> lege, and scraped the hard bone of pride. . . . With those
> three words, she had indirectly told me what the Catho-
> lic Worker Movement is all about and what she herself
> was like.[6]

During the years he knew her, Coles would learn many things
from Dorothy Day, but this particular lesson would serve as a basis
for everything else. Dorothy's use of the words "one of us" placed
the ranting, alcoholic woman on a par with herself, and, for that
moment at least, clothed her with respect. That afternoon in the
Catholic Worker house, Dorothy and her companion were, to use
Gerald May's phrase, two notes in the human symphony—one
harmonious and one discordant, one sweet and one harsh, but
both part of the same song. Dorothy was, like Caryll Houselander
and Thomas Merton, possessed by a conviction of the presence of
Christ in everyone. It was this certainty of his radiant love alive

---

6. Coles, *Dorothy Day*, xviii.

in every person that compelled her to live in service of that love, regardless of how unlikely or unattractive a vessel she might find it.

Caryll Houselander noted that at times she could only keep alive the vision of Christ's presence in others through "a deliberate and blind act of faith." Dorothy Day and Thomas Merton also knew what it was to live on faith. Rainer Maria Rilke wrote to his young poet friend that "the demands which the difficult work of love makes upon our development are more than life-size, and as beginners we are not up to them."[7] We are, he felt, "apprentices" to the demands of love. For most of us, it is an apprenticeship that never ends, but it is one that is built on a solid and certain foundation. Although living very different lifestyles, this foundation was the same one on which Caryll Houselander, Thomas Merton, Dorothy Day, and countless others have built their lives and learned to live as disciples and friends.

PRINCIPLE OF CREATIVE LOVE

For most of us, it is difficult to trust that we are truly loved, and to trust that the intimacy we all crave is already there for us. We often live as if we have to earn love, do something noteworthy, and then perhaps we might get something in return.

However, this attitude touches on the *principle of creative love* in the spiritual life. This is the belief we are *loved first*, independent of what we do or accomplish. The reason this is so important is because as long as we think we have to earn God's love, that we have to "become good" first, we can actually hinder receiving what we most desire: a love that cannot be earned, but that is freely given.

St. John the Evangelist wrote in his First Letter that we are able to love because God has first loved us (1 John 4:19). William Barry says we are precious with a value far beyond our comprehension, and we have been created not out of any need God has *of* us but because of his overflowing love *for* us.[8] We are created for no other

7. Rilke, *Letters to a Young Poet*, 57.
8. Barry, *God's Passionate Desire*, 99.

reason than that we are deeply wanted by God. It is this indelible imprint of God's passion within us that is the fundamental yearning we all have—the "terrific thing," the "unquenchable fire" deep within us. He desires a relationship with each of us and approaches us in faithful, inexhaustible love. He loves us first, freely and extravagantly. His love for us creates the love within each of us that draws us out of ourselves to love one another. We are offered no less than the constancy of his abiding presence in a relationship "of ever-increasing intimacy and love . . . most fittingly described as friendship."[9]

BEING ON THE GUEST LIST

Scott Peck defines mystics as those wonderfully aware people among us who have a sensitively developed consciousness of an invisible interconnectedness beneath the surface of things.[10] Like all gifts coming from God's Spirit, their mystical sensitivity is given to them for the good of many others. The English anchoress and mystic Julian of Norwich was graced in her life with a series of visions that seemed to reveal the depths of God's mystery and wonder. In one such showing she received an exquisite vision of a heavenly feast.

> My mind was lifted up to heaven, and I saw Our Lord as a lord in his own house, where He had called his much loved friends to a banquet. I saw that the Lord did not sit in one place, but ranged throughout the house, filling it with joy and gladness. Completely relaxed and courteous, he was Himself the happiness and peace of his dear friends, his beautiful face radiating measureless love like a marvelous symphony; and it was that wonderful face shining with the beauty of God that filled that heavenly place with joy and light.[11]

9. Wadell, *Friendship and the Moral Life*, 207.

10. Peck, *A World Waiting to be Born*, 20.

11. Rees, "A Woman in Love with God," 59.

This showing of Julian's is much more than a privileged revelation received centuries ago by an obscure medieval woman; it is a delicately beautiful image still able to teach across time of the reality of the feast of love to which we are all invited. In Julian's vision, the Lord has called his friends to join him, and in his graciousness he moves among them in such perfect communion that he himself is their deepest joy and consolation. The Lord of the banquet is the Lord of our lives, and we are the "dear friends" he invites into the unending gladness of his own house. In fact, the name of each one of us is on the guest list because all of us have been given the gift of our identity in Christ deep within what George Aschenbrenner calls the "deepest core of the soul."[12] In this deepest core of ourselves we simply *are*, and it is this profound identity that unites us in all our diversity, giving each of us a "still point in the ever turning world of our own person."[13]

Utilizing a similar metaphor, C. S. Lewis says that friends on our spiritual journey are envoys of the overflowing grace an attentive God lavishes on us. As such, they are not chance acquaintances but gifts given to us by God.

> Christ, who said to his disciples "You have not chosen me, but I have chosen you," can truly say to every group of Christian friends "You have not chosen one another but I have chosen you for one another." The friendship is not a reward for our discrimination and good taste in finding one another out. It is the instrument by which God reveals to each the beauties of all the others. . . . They are, like all beauties, derived from Him, and then, in a good friendship, increased by Him. . . . At this feast it is He who has spread the board and it is He who has chosen the guests.[14]

For Lewis, the torrent of God's love "running through life" links us not only to him but to every other person. The Lord who is *in* us is also *between* us, not to single us out and to separate

---

12. Aschenbrenner, "A Hidden Self Grown Strong," 231.

13. Ibid., 234.

14. Lewis, *The Four Loves*, 126–27.

us from each other but to bind us closer together in friendship. Loving as Jesus loves us first is to be a great dynamic of generosity in which "the new is always breaking in" to push us past the confines of our self-imposed boundaries.[15] Each of us is in a constant process of becoming who we are meant to be in Christ, and only in relationship with each other can we hope to grow in that identity. The friendships given to us in our spiritual life call from us an investment of self and a commitment to the risk, change, growth, challenge, and joy of intimate, mutual companionship. We are not competitors but partners in a "sacred connection" in which each friend affirms the "be-ing" of the other.[16] It is in our faithfulness to the commitment we make to such a relationship that we mirror God's unwavering fidelity and we start to become the person Jesus commands us to be.

15. Jones, *Exploring Spiritual Direction*, 62.
16. O'Donohue, *Anam Cara*, 19.

4

Teachers on Friendship

CLASSICAL WRITERS: LAYING THE FOUNDATION

Aristotle: "Choosing Nobility"

The topic of friendship has been written about by both Christian and non-Christian writers for centuries. For example, Aristotle devoted so much attention to the subject of friendship in his *Nichomachean Ethics* and a comparable amount of space in his *Eudemian Ethics*, which would suggest that friendship was very important to understanding his moral philosophy. Nevertheless, many of the studies of Aristotle's ethics focuses on other areas, and his books on friendship suffer almost universal neglect. This is unfortunate for two reasons. First of all, Aristotle's concept of happiness, the end towards which all human action is ordered, contains friendship as an integral part. His analysis of what is requisite for a person's fulfillment leads Aristotle to conclude that no one can be called happy who does not experience friendship.[1] Consequently, neglect of Aristotle's lengthy discussion of friendship can hinder a person's understanding of the goal established by his moral philosophy.

Secondly, it is in Aristotle's doctrine of friendship that one finds admirably reconciled the apparent duality of one's strivings toward self-perfection with one's nature as a social being. The good person is one with the true friend, so that to fail to appreciate the role of friendship in Aristotle is to lack understanding of virtue in operation. It is, after all, in the activities of virtuous friends that we discover the most sublime reaches of human potential.

Aristotle's division of friendship into three kinds, which occurs early in Book VIII of his *Nichomachean Ethics*, gives immediate indication of the non-egocentric nature of friendship in its truest form. Friendship of utility and friendship of pleasure differ from friendship of virtue inasmuch as the former love "for the sake of what is good in themselves" (1156a15). If a friend is loved because he is pleasant or useful, this friendship will eventually dissolve when this service to self is no longer needed or available. Even vicious people can enjoy friendships of these sorts. Virtue is not required, for example, if friends are such because of their usefulness to one another in business deals. The same is true when pleasure is the object, as when one values a friend because he is a good drinking companion. By contrast, true friendship can exist only between good people, and the distinguishing characteristic of this kind of friendship is that the friend is loved for his own sake (1156b9). The object of love possesses goodness and therefore what is loved in the friend is intrinsic rather than incidental.

Of course, goodness or virtue may vary from individual to individual. Hence, even within friendships of virtue (character friendships), there will be differences of degree and friends of this sort are prepared to assist one another in the growth of virtue. However, one must keep in mind the purpose of this assistance,

---

1. "For without friends no one would choose to love, though he had all other goods," Aristotle, *Ethica Nichomachea*, VII, 1, 1155a5. Hereafter, all quotations from Aristotle will be immediately followed by Bekker numbers for purposes of locating passages in the Ross translation.

"for in purpose lies the essential element of virtue and character" (1163a23). Love and friendship of the finest sort wills the other's good for the sake of the other. This is why true friendship gives so little cause for complaint. Who can complain of a friend who wills the other's good? Lesser friendships are full of complaints because "they use each other for their own interests" and each wants "to get the better of the bargain" (1162b16).

Noble friendship rises above such wrangling, for the essence of this relationship consists in loving rather than in being loved (1159a33). What is of value in lesser friendships is not sacrificed in noble friendship, however, inasmuch as "the good man is at the same time pleasant and useful" (1158a33). Delighting in the admirable qualities of the beloved, noble friends naturally wish to spend their time in one another's company, since "there is nothing so characteristic of friends as living together" (1157b19). Preferring the companionship of one another to everything else, the utility of noble friendship is also clear. A friend seeks to transfer to himself the traits he admires in the other, and in this case they are truly admirable. Therefore, it is in association with a virtuous friend that one grows in virtue. The good will of that virtuous friend is unquestionable, because his character requires he seek others to be the object of his beneficence. The subtle reconciliation of self-love and love for another reveals itself once again. The "good person will need people to do well by" (1169b14). Consequently, in conferring benefits upon another he is satisfying his own needs.

In chapter eight of Book IX, Aristotle directly tackles the problem of egoism. "The question is also debated," he says, "whether a man should love himself most, or some one else" (1168a28). He responds to this question with a distinction. The prevailing type of self-love is rightly a matter of reproach. For, lovers of self in the bad sense "assign to themselves the greater share of wealth, honors and bodily pleasure" (1168b16). However, the true lover of self, unlike most men, will assign to himself "the things that are noblest and best" (1168b29). The good person wishes to excel in virtuous deeds. What are objects of competition for most people are of no consequence to him. He gladly dispenses with these in order that he may accomplish that which is finest in his nature. What the good person wants to do in life is identical with what a person, morally speaking, ought to do. It follows that a good person should be a lover of self, for his nature is lovable. In fulfilling his wants, which are to perform noble acts, he simultaneously profits himself and benefits others.

It is no mystery, then, why a good person will sacrifice so much for his friend. He identifies his own good with the good of the one whom he loves. This unselfishness is exhibited, first of all, in the willingness to share material possessions. "What friends have is common property" (1168b7). But it extends beyond this. Good persons make the best friends, because in each there is so much that is worthy of love. The things of which they approve are the same. Whether in times of good fortune or in times of adversity, friends will seek out one another, for they are prepared to share sorrows as well as joys. What strikes the egoist as most paradoxical, the willingness of a noble person even to die for the sake of his friend, presents no problem to Aristotle. It has already been established that the good person loves in himself the disposition to virtuous acts. Therefore, he will choose nobility before all else. If circumstances require that his life be lost in the service of those he loves, then a good person will choose the greater prize. In sacrificing his life for his friend, he assigns to himself nobility (1169a18–36).

Living out this doctrine of friendship might be judged by some as unacceptable or even impossible of implementation. This would not be surprising to Aristotle. Fundamental to his ethical theory is the conviction that people's habits determine what they find desirable. The sources of pleasure to a good person differ from those of an evil person. Ideal friendship will not attract a person lacking in those qualities by which Aristotle defines virtuous living. And, indeed, it must be conceded that for some individuals it is not possible to be a noble friend. Aristotle would argue that unselfish friendship is an eligible good only for those properly disposed.

Aristotle also maintained that "as a man is to himself, so is he to his friend" (1171b32). If an individual does not find his own being desirable, he will not be able to find a friend's being desirable. Now, some people have good reason not to love themselves. A lovable self is created through the cultivation of praiseworthy qualities. However, even those persons who are properly disposed for noble friendship will not possess many persons as their friends. It is Aristotle's belief that love, an emotion of affection carried to a point of intensity, can only be felt for one or at most a few. A considerable investment of time and attention is made in acquiring experience of the other and becoming familiar with him or her. Finally, the intimate manner of their living together, sharing so completely their interests, their joys, and their griefs, means that "great friendship can only be felt toward a few people," and that "the famous friendships of this sort are always between two people" (1171a13–15).

Some people believe this kind of noble friendship as described by Aristotle could only be understood by one who has had this experience. Even the reader of Aristotle's account of friendship might be skeptical unless that person too has shared a similar experience. Nevertheless, Aristotle's understanding of friendship establishes the possibility of genuine unselfishness in human relationships. It is this understanding of friendship that has influenced much of the development of friendship in Christian spirituality.

Cicero: Friendship: "Looking at Yourself in the Mirror"

M. Tullius Cicero (106–43 BC) was a Roman orator, philosopher, and political leader. His book *Laelius: De Amicitia* develops the theme of friendship in classical terms and has been very influential in the spirituality of Western Christian writers. Relying upon Greek philosophers, such as Plato and Aristotle, who preceded him, Cicero describes friendship in his treatise as the most important and attractive human bond between people, one based on the common pursuit of virtue, not financial profit, flattery, or sensuality:

> Friendship may be defined as a complete identity of feel-
> ing with all things in heaven and earth: an identity which
> is strengthened by mutual good will and affection. With
> the single exception of wisdom, I am inclined to regard
> it as the greatest of all the gifts the gods have bestowed
> upon mankind.[2]

Cicero also associates friendship with trust and hope and he
identifies friendship with looking at yourself in the mirror. He felt
that true friendship would create a certain kind of freedom within
a person that would allow a person to feel comfortable sharing
anything with his or her friend. In this sense, a friend is like having someone who knows you so well that it is like having a "second
self."

> It is the most satisfying experience in the world to have
> someone you can speak to as freely as your own self
> about any and every subject upon earth. . . . When a man
> thinks of a true friend, he is looking at himself in the
> mirror. Even when a friend is absent, he is present all
> the same.[3]

Friendship (*amicitia* in Latin) derives, Cicero believed, from
the Latin word for love (*amor*). It "comes from a feeling of affection," he says, "an inclination of the heart." For Cicero, the significance of friendship is that it unites human hearts. Because of this,
"authentic friendship is permanent;" it cannot and will not die.[4]

Cicero also linked friendship with "a mutual belief in each
other's goodness,"[5] and certainly a great deal of mutual affection.
"Friendships . . . are formed when an exemplar of shining goodness
makes itself manifest, and when some congenial spirit feels the desire to fasten on to this model. Then the result will be affection."[6]

Finally, Cicero believed wisdom (*sapientia*) was the virtue
that creates and maintains friendships. Without wisdom, he felt

2. Sellner, "An Inclination of the Heart," 164.

3. Ibid.

4. Grant, *Cicero*, 179.

5. Ibid., 197.

6. Ibid., 203.

people would be more likely to choose friends who might be unhealthy in a variety of ways, and it would be extremely difficult to maintain this kind of friendship over a long period of time.

CHRISTIAN SPIRITUAL WRITERS

In our Christian tradition, we believe we are the newest faces of a long line of those who are ardently seeking God and his saving grace. Those who have gone before us have had the same yearnings, the same longings we do, and in a legacy of great richness, they have left behind a record of what they came to understand about God through their own personal experiences and in their relationships with others. We certainly have a relationship with these people, their ideas, and their experiences and we can learn a great deal from them about the importance of friendship in the spiritual life.

In Christian spirituality, our tradition exists for us as a place to learn from the triumphs, insights, struggles, and questions of those who have gone before us. We can turn to them "in search of language, metaphors, insight and direction," which can greatly enrich the spiritual journey of each of us.[7] In John's Gospel, Jesus called the disciples his friends and appointed them to go and bear fruit that would remain (John 15:15–16). Over the centuries, countless numbers of his other friends have taken that commission seriously, and we are the fortunate beneficiaries of their loving friendship with Christ.

The record emerging from the church's tradition contains classic writings that can be "read and reread with profit from generation to generation."[8] These holy men and women described, to the best of their ability, their consuming love and dedication to God. The five teachers who will be considered here—St. Jerome, St. Aelred of Rievaulx, St. Teresa of Avila, St. Thomas Aquinas, and St. Francis de Sales—knew a great deal about the sacred link between

7. Dreyer, *Earth Crammed with Heaven*, 37.
8. Ibid.

love of God and love for others. Their insights into the value of friendship in the spiritual life contain a richness from which we can learn how to cultivate lasting friendships that reflect the love of God.

St. Jerome. Friend: "Half of One's Soul"

One of the great spiritual and intellectual leaders of the early Christian Church was Eusebius Hieronymus or, as we have come to know him, St. Jerome. Born around 340 AD at Strido near Aquileia, a village on the Adriatic coast, he studied as a youth in Rome where he was baptized and then traveled to Gaul with a friend, Bonosus, before devoting himself to experiments in monasticism. This new form of Christian life was becoming increasingly popular as a result of the stories, trickling back to the West, of the desert fathers and mothers who were acting as spiritual guides. In imitation of those early heroes, Jerome lived with a group of friends in Aquileia, and when that community broke apart he set out in 374 to live a more solitary life. After a brief stay in Antioch he settled as a hermit in the Syrian desert of Chalcis. Unhappy and unsatisfied for a variety of reasons, he eventually moved back to Antioch where he was ordained a priest, traveled to Constantinople, and from 382–385 was in Rome where he served as a secretary to Pope Damasus.

In Rome, he functioned as a spiritual director to numerous lay people, especially women. Three of these women were particularly important to him. Marcella was a wealthy Roman widow; Paula, another widow; and her daughter, Eustochium. Of the three, the latter two eventually joined him in Bethlehem where in 386 he established a monastic community, one that expressed his own ascetic ideals and provided him, at last, some degree of happiness.

Jerome was a man of fiery temperament. Although one biographer calls him the patron saint of "ill-tempered people," he was also known for his friendships and for his spiritual direction.[9]

9. Steinmann, *Saint Jerome and His Times*, 4.

Much of this side of Jerome is revealed in his letters, which, according to the Cistercian scholar Jean Leclercq, were "models of the art of letter writing and a source for ideals on monastic asceticism."[10]

Through these numerous letters, as well as his Scripture commentaries, hagiographies, and especially his translation of the Bible into Latin (subsequently known as The Vulgate), Jerome had a tremendous influence on the development of Christianity in the West. Moreover, his letters give us insight into his understanding of friendship, especially as they relate to the three women just mentioned who became his lifelong friends. Jerome's great capacity for friendship was precisely what formed the basis of his own significant ministry as a spiritual director. Furthermore, this ability to make friends and his work as a spiritual guide, among other ministries, tend to make Jerome's considerable personality flaws more tolerable.

If anything can be discerned in Jerome's writings, it is that his passion for friendship, with both men and women, was matched only by his passion for books.[11] His letters betray an exceptionally needy man, one who is deeply hurt and quickly angered when his friends fail to live up to his expectations of them: to write back to him, to visit him, to stay with him, or to return his affection. In one of his early letters (11), he writes to "the virgins of Haemona" from his retreat in the desert of Chalcis: "But now, I beg you, pardon me for having a grievance. I am saying it because I am hurt. I say it in tears and in anger: you have not addressed a single syllable to one who so often bestows his affection on you."[12] In another letter (12), he addresses Antonius, a monk living in the same area:

> Ten times already, if I am not mistaken, have I sent you letters full of kindness and entreaties. But you do not deign to utter even a grunt, and though the Lord spoke with His slaves, you, a brother, do not speak with your brother. . . . But as it is human to become angry and Christian to abstain from harm, I return to my old way:

10. Leclercq, *Love of Learning*, 97.

11. Kelly, *Jerome*, 20.

12. Jerome, *Letters of Saint Jerome*, 53.

> I entreat you once more to love me as I love you and, as a
> fellow servant (of Christ), speak to your fellow servant.[13]

In effect, Jerome wanted his friends to love him as he needed to be loved. His correspondence shows that, along with a keen intellect, he had strong emotions and was definitely not afraid of expressing them. What he wrote about St. Paul the Apostle could apply to himself as well: "Wherever you look, the lightening is flashing."[14] For whatever reason, his writings reflect great passion and his great need for love.

No one work on friendship can be found in Jerome's writings, no unified statement explaining his theory of friendship or its practice. His opinions on the topic, however, emerge in the 150 letters of his that survived. What becomes clear is how much he thinks and speaks of friendship in classical terms, especially as reflected in the writings of Cicero. Cicero's *Laelius: De Amicitia*, in particular, is quoted frequently by Jerome in his own writings, suggesting how much his theology of friendship was influenced by the Roman writer.

When Jerome speaks of friendship he often uses Ciceronian images and phrases. A friend, according to Jerome, is half of one's soul and an alter ego, another self.[15] As he says in a letter to St. Augustine, a correspondent who shared with him a profound appreciation of friendships, "Friendship ought to be free from all suspicion and one should be able to talk to a friend as to a second self."[16] These references to friendship as consisting of two bodies sharing one soul or to a friend as a second self are found in numerous classical writings, and Jerome would have been familiar with many of them.[17] Like Cicero, Jerome also believed in the permanence of friendship, echoing the Roman writer's words when he states in an early letter to Rufinus "a friend is long sought, is rarely

13. Ibid., 55–56.

14. Steinmann, *Saint Jerome and His Times*, 226.

15. Jerome, *Letters of Saint Jerome*, 31.

16. White, *The Correspondence*, 95.

17. White, *Christian Friendship in the Fourth Century*, 21.

come upon, and is hard to keep. . . . Friendship that can cease was never real."[18]

Differences, however, can be found between Cicero's classical philosophy and Jerome's Christian theology of friendship. While Cicero suggested that *sapientia* (wisdom) was the virtue that created and maintained friendships, Jerome believed friendship was not only closely tied with wisdom but with the activity and work of Christ. In Letter 5, he says to Florentinus, "though absent in person, I do come to you in love and in spirit, earnestly beseeching you that no extent of time or space may tear asunder our growing friendship, cemented as it is in Christ."[19]

Christ then was the cement, the glue that bound friends together, and therefore every Christian friendship consisted not of just two persons, but three. As Jerome explains in a letter (60) to his longtime friend, Heliodorus, such relationships transcend geographical distance and the passage of time. "We write letters and send replies, our messages cross the seas, and as the ship cleaves a furrow through the waves the moments we have to live grow less. We have but one profit: we are joined together by the love of Christ."[20]

While Cicero used a mirror as a metaphor for friendship, Jerome compared friendship to an open door. In a letter (145) to Exuperantius, a Roman soldier whom he invited to live with him in Bethlehem, he wrote, "I have knocked at the door of friendship: if you open it to me, you will find me a frequent visitor."[21]

From his extant letters, as well as from numerous prefaces to his scriptural commentaries, we know that besides the male friends whom he loved, and with whom he frequently fought, Jerome loved women, beginning with his grandmother from whose arms, he says, he was torn and dragged off to school as a child.[22] However, Elizabeth Clark maintains that "his relations with

18. Jerome, *Letters of Saint Jerome*, 34.

19. Ibid., 37.

20. Jerome, *Select Letters*, 309.

21. Fremantle, "Principle Works of St. Jerome," 288.

22. Monceaux, *St. Jerome*, 13.

women remain to this day somewhat of a puzzle. For example, he confessed his love for them yet warned clerics against associating with them."[23] But Jerome's own feelings were probably just as mysterious to him, if not more so. Perhaps he loved women too much. Perhaps this is why he seemed to distance himself by adopting a paternalistic, highly critical, and at times outright hostile attitude toward them. Possibly he did this in order to protect himself from his own passionate nature, as well as the rumors from his detractors that he paid too much attention to women. Reflecting on this interior struggle, J. N. D. Kelly says, "strongly sexed but also, because of his convictions, strongly repressed as well, his nature craved for female society and found deep satisfaction in it when it could be had without doing violence to his principles."[24]

Jerome alludes to some of his struggles with eros in his letters: he confesses he was not a virgin, and that while in the desert of Chalcis visions of dancing girls filled his cell. Despite his extreme ascetical practices there, he says "the fires of the passions kept boiling within me."[25] Even when he was much older, he spoke of "that uniquely burdensome tyrant, sexual desire," which he compared, as Augustine did, to fire.[26] No wonder he would disagree with men like Evagrius of Pontus who believed that *apatheia*, a state of inner harmony, was a worthy and attainable goal. Based on his own experience, Jerome thought such a state impossible except, he says, if one were a stone or God.[27]

Jerome identifies himself with Mary Magdalene, the sinful but contrite woman who washes Jesus's feet with her tears (Luke 7: 39). This is quite revealing of his inner state and his ongoing struggles with eros. He gives us a clue to how he handles his erotic energies when he tells the young virgin, Eustochium, "it is hard for the human soul not to love, and it is necessary that our mind be

23. Clark, *Jerome, Chrysostom, and Friends*, 45.

24. Kelly, *Jerome*, 91.

25. Jerome, *Letters of St. Jerome*, 140.

26. Kelly, *Jerome*, 295.

27. Ramsey, *John Cassian*, 19.

drawn into some sort of affection. Love of the flesh is overcome by love of the spirit. Desire is quenched by desire."[28]

Jerome's affection and his desires seem to have been sublimated into his ministry, especially spiritual direction. This was precisely what he did when he left the desert and moved to Rome. There his life revolved around the aristocratic men and women of the Aventine whom he counseled and taught, and with whom he corresponded. They frequently met with Jerome in prayer, study, and care of the poor. What brought them together was what Cicero links with friendship—"a mutual belief in each other's goodness."[29]

Jerome died September 30 in 419 or 420, resting at last from a full, highly productive life. In the years following his death Jerome's fame increased steadily, taking on legendary proportions. By the eighth century, he, along with Ambrose, Augustine, and Gregory the Great, was declared a "Doctor of the Church," the first of many to be honored for their spiritual leadership and significant theological contributions.[30]

St. Aelred of Rievaulx. Friend: "A Kindred Spirit"

Like Jerome, on first consideration, it may seem the life and writings of someone as removed from the present day as the twelfth century abbot Aelred (1110–1167) would be of limited interest. Yet in the prologue of his work *Spiritual Friendship*, he introduces himself and his intentions in such a way as to make him seem quite recognizable to anyone who, following a conversion, has worked to integrate what is most precious and significant into a new framework of understanding. The young Aelred, naturally inclined toward affection and fellowship, found in Cicero's classic writing on friendship a standard by which he could measure the "vacillations" of his own relationships.[31] After he entered the

28. Jerome, *Letters of St. Jerome*, 149.

29. Grant, *Cicero*, 197.

30. McGinn, *The Doctors of the Church*, 88.

31. Aelred of Rievaulx, *Spiritual Friendship*, 46.

monastery, however, Cicero as a guide was no longer sufficient. Having given himself to Christ, Aelred found that "nothing which had not been sweetened by the honey of the most sweet name of Jesus, nothing which had not been seasoned with the salt of sacred scripture" could draw him.[32] Unable to rely solely on Cicero and yet feeling inadequate to attain the exalted friendships the saints knew, he decided to write on the subject himself in an effort to set down the "rules for a chaste and holy love" that were true to the Christian life.[33]

Written over the space of twenty years and constructed in the form of a dialogue, Aelred's *Spiritual Friendship* stands in the tradition as possibly "the most important Christian text on friendship as holiness."[34] For Aelred, the foundation of this holiness was to be found in the love of God, and therefore distinctions were to be made among kinds of friendship. There were, he realized, associations whose common bond was for purposes of vice or for advantage in position of profit. While these might be called "friendships," that identification was falsely applied to them. Even those who might love each other through ties of family or in the fellowship of a common cause might not be friends. A true friend, Aelred believed, needed to be "chosen with the upmost care and tested with extreme caution," for this person was to be a partner in the love of God—a kindred spirit who was to be an intimate companion of one's soul."[35] He wrote:

> But what happiness, what security, what joy to have someone to whom you dare to speak on terms of equality as to another self; one to whom you need have no fear to confess your failings; one to whom you can unblushingly make known what progress you have made in the spiritual life; one to whom you can entrust all the secrets of your heart and before whom you can place all you

32. Ibid.
33. Ibid., 47.
34. Cunningham and Egan, *Christian Spirituality*, 171.
35. Aelred of Rievaulx, *Spiritual Friendship*, 93.

> plans! What, therefore, is more pleasant than . . . to unite
> oneself to the spirit of another and of two to form one.[36]

In Aelred's understanding, friendships that were worthy of
the name were not built around motives for any material thing
because they could not sustain themselves against the extreme
variability of fortune. A friendship of true value in the spiritual life
was one of affection and steadfast loyalty in which the temptations
of envy, ambition, and personal gain were ineffective. It was to be
sought "on account of God and for its own sake,"[37] and the growth
in perfection of the friends together—in "honor and charm, truth
and joy, sweetness and good-will, affection and action"—was to be
the only measure of progress.[38] A friendship that was holy needed
to be centered around eternal values and not transitory temporal
ones, and a truly spiritual friendship, grounded in the love of God
and patterned after the example of Christ, was never meant to end.

In the abundance of creation, God left nothing to exist alone.
The pattern of the created order, Aelred believed, was toward the
unity of each thing with its own kind; human beings, made from
the very substance of each other, were designed for the mutuality
of friendship. Jesus called us his friends (John 15:15) and drew us
to himself in a bond of great intimacy. It is his love that is the model
and inspiration for the love exchanged between friends. "Friend
cleaving to friend in the spirit of Christ is made with Christ but
one heart and one soul," and all the goodness and growth friends
enjoy together "take their beginning from Christ, advance through
Christ, and are perfected in Christ."[39] For Aelred, this was the
strength and authenticity of a holy and true friendship, pointing
toward even greater fullness to come. Spiritual friends growing together
were destined to move beyond present adversities and even
death itself to the bright eternity of friendship without end, where

36. Ibid., 72.
37. Ibid., 107.
38. Ibid., 74.
39. Ibid., 74–75.

all would be forever united in and with the God who had drawn them to love each other through him.

St. Teresa of Avila. Friend: A Shield for One Another

Teresa (1515–1582), like Aelred, was a person dedicated to the monastic life, and she is rightly known as a woman of great mystical gifts whose rich legacy is her teaching on the interior life of prayer. Friendship as a topic, however, appears in various places in her writings, because she knew through the trials of her own experience that the spiritual life could not be lived in isolation. It is small wonder that this remarkable woman, who knew the joy of transforming union with God, would have a great overflow of love to share with the cherished friends who were her companions on the journey home to him.

Teresa was a passionate woman who possessed a keen intelligence and a sharp sense of practicality. She had a personality that was filled with wit, charm, and affection, and she was favored with a physical attractiveness, which, combined with her other traits, made her immensely appealing. She wrote simply of this as a fact in her autobiography, stating plainly "everywhere I was always loved."[40] Throughout her busy and demanding life, she worked at understanding the importance human love and friendships should have for anyone dedicated to God. She was by nature an intensely relational person, but she wished to avoid what she regarded as the mistakes of her earlier life. Therefore, as she grew in her love of God, she brought all of her friendships into the transforming power of that primary relationship.[41] Her love for others increased as she came to love God more, and she wrote that "it is necessary for those who serve Him to become shields for one another" in order to support each other against the temptations and criticisms of the many who had no desire to lead holy lives.[42]

---

40. Teresa of Avila, *Collected Works*, 62.
41. Wicks, "Teresa of Avila," 116.
42. Teresa of Avila, *Collected Works*, 93.

It can be said of Teresa that for her "a person's degree of immersion in God was the degree of her love for that person."[43] She cautioned her sisters in *The Way of Perfection* against the factionalism exclusive, possessive friendships could cause in the community, and she counseled that "all must love and like and help one another" in order to be of greatest benefit for spiritual progress.[44] Teresa had confidence that the Lord who moved her to love would also rightly direct the focus of her friendships. She trusted that she and all those vowed to a life of prayer would be prevented "from becoming attached to anyone who does not serve God fervently."[45] Yet she knew that deep lovers of God were the ones capable of loving others not less but "far more, with a truer, more generous and passionate affection."[46] Teresa wrote:

> If they care for anyone, their eyes are not arrested by the body but at once look into the soul to see if it contains aught they can love . . . loving this soul, no trouble wearies them, no service is too hard for them willing to render it, as they wish their affection for it to last, which they know is impossible unless their friend possesses virtue and loves God greatly.[47]

The bond between two friends sincerely loving God together was so secure, Teresa felt, that it could withstand correction when it was necessary. A person possessing a friend who could offer loving criticism was truly blessed because the heart of such a companion would "never deal falsely by those it loves . . . if it sees them go astray . . . it warns them of it immediately. It cannot resist doing so, nor can it flatter its friends nor dissemble their faults."[48] Egocentricity had no place in Teresa's concept of true friendship but the shared desire for mutual spiritual growth did. In her mind, friends

---

43. Dubay, *Fire Within*, 273.
44. Teresa of Avila, *Way of Perfection*, 22–23.
45. Ibid., 27.
46. Ibid., 36.
47. Ibid.
48. Ibid., 40.

needed to be selfless enough to desire the good of the other as well as humble enough to accept loving correction when it was offered.

"The company of God's friends is a good way of keeping near Him," Teresa observed, and it was because her friendships were centered in God that they enjoyed "the security of tenderness, patience, durability and permanence."[49] Gifted with sublime mystical experiences, she was also able to fully appreciate the joy of human relationships. Throughout her active life, she put herself at the disposal of divine love, and it was as special gifts of divine love that she believed her friendships were such a support and a blessing to a deeply lived spiritual life.

St. Thomas Aquinas. Friend: A Treasured Companion

In his book on the masters and teachers of spirituality, Bishop Alfred Hughes wrote that the growing realization of God's ever-present love for us can touch us in the depths of our being. If we allow it, this realization will ignite a spark within us that can become "more and more a driving force in our lives."[50] This energy moves us from self-centeredness to ever deeper engagement with God and others, and this process of transformation—open to every person—was what the great theologian Thomas Aquinas (1225–1274) felt the Christian life was all about. Our acceptance of the grace of God's love is the foundation of our friendship with him, and Thomas called that friendship "charity."[51]

We are able to enter into friendship with God, Thomas believed, only because God graciously shares his very life and love with us, thereby making it possible for us to love him in return. This is a tremendous gift, Thomas noted, that we have "neither by nature, nor as acquired, but as infused by the Holy Spirit, who is the love of the Father and the Son."[52] Our response to this gift of

49. Dubay, *Fire Within*, 283.

50. Hughes, *Spiritual Masters*, 47–48.

51. Wadell, *Friendship and the Moral Life*, 206.

52. Ibid., 207.

charity-friendship is to allow it to ever more deeply change us—to let it become, as Hughes phrased it, a "drawing force" in our lives. All that we do—whether great or small—can then be directed to God as a reflection of our loving friendship with him. "Being patient with one another, serving one another, forgiving one another, caring for one another, supporting one another" become the outward signs of a life of charity that is other-centered, because the gift of friendship God gives to each is meant to be shared among all.

Friendship with God is offered to every person individually, but it is not meant as a narrow and exclusive possession. We are linked through the grace of charity with every other person, and the challenge we have is to move into the world of another and to learn to respond to others in a way that leads to communion and enrichment. For Thomas, our relationships were extensions and expressions of the depth of our friendship with God. There were, however, specific others with whom we would share the mutuality and intimacy that came from the common desire to live in holiness. These spiritual friends were those who encouraged and supported one another in the gospel life and in the nurturing of virtues such as "generosity, justice, compassion, patience, perseverance, forgiveness, courage, faithfulness, and joy."[53] Through the bond of charity, spiritual friends recognized one another as treasured companions in understanding what was meant by a life in God and what was needed in living faithfully to it.

Thomas believed the most crucial element in faithfulness to friendship with God was a commitment to follow the example of Jesus his Son. Jesus was for him the ultimate offering of friendship to a broken and separated human race as well as the perfect model of creation. God gave us Jesus as the pattern in the very beginning when we were created for love, compassion, and goodness; we can understand what friendship with God is only through Jesus' "attitudes and virtues . . . his teaching and ministry, and especially . . . his total openness to God's will."[54] Thomas called Jesus the

53. Ibid., 209.
54. Ibid., 212.

"path" to life in God, and a person seeking to come to the fullness of charity could only find the way "through a participation in the Word of God, even as the pupil makes progress by receiving the teacher's word."[55]

The progress of the "pupils" of Christ extends over a lifetime because we are invited to renew daily our commitment of discipleship to him. By hearing Christ's words, by learning from his example, and by receiving him through the sacramental life of the church, especially the Eucharist, Thomas felt we are indeed made new creatures in every dimension of our being. Adherence to Christ who was the perfection of friendship with the Father makes us true friends of God, and in the fullness of charity, we are called to be witnesses of the "joy, peace, mercy, kindness, almsgiving, and fraternal correction" characteristic of those who live close to God.[56] Spiritual friends, in Thomas' understanding, had a mission that went beyond the sanctification they might experience together and the unity they would know in their love and support for each other. They had a ministry of sanctification to bring to the whole world. By the example of their devotion and through the conduct of their lives, they were to present to others the possibility of an existence that was open to everyone. It is a world that can come into being when we remember who we are meant to be—friends of God who have accepted his gracious offer of friendship and invite others to "a way of life together that is blessed and full of hope."[57]

St. Francis de Sales. Friend: "Bright Mirror" of God

Three hundred years after the time of St. Thomas Aquinas, the Bishop of Geneva, Francis de Sales (1567–1622) spent part of his considerable energy writing a series of directions and meditations that received widespread publication. This work, *Introduction to a*

55. Ibid., 212–13.
56. Ibid., 215.
57. Ibid.

Devout Life, was addressed not to those in monasteries or convents but to "all who aspire to devotion," to anyone "loving, or in love with, God."[58] Francis defined devotion as the grace of divine love at work in the soul, strengthening one to open his or her life to do what is good "carefully, frequently, and promptly."[59] Devout men and women in every vocation brought the love of God into the world as they faithfully carried out the duties of their daily lives. God was present in the ordinary events and common activities of the everyday, and those persons dedicated to devotion constantly grew in their appreciation of the gift of God's love overflowing into all of life.

This particular way of seeing is best described as contemplative awareness; devout souls sensed the interconnectedness of all things and lived profoundly influenced by such an understanding. The goal of a life of devotion as Francis conceived it was a re-orientation of the whole person toward God—a shaping of the entire way in which an individual approached the concrete realities of daily life. In his preface to the *Introduction* he stated, "I neither can nor will, nor indeed should I write . . . anything but what has already been published by our predecessors on the same subject."[60] Like those who came before him, Francis believed love was "the fundamental principle of our humanity and the realization of our deepest nature."[61] With his predecessors, he understood that the whole of the Christian life was a transformation of the person into a new creation in Christ. His particular gift was his ability to present these truths in a manner that was accessible to people in all walks of life, and his special grace was the way he lived these truths in all the dimensions of his own life, especially his friendships.

Francis, as bishop, teacher, spiritual director, and friend was "a man imbued with the love of God and desirous of sharing that love with all who would seek it."[62] To live a life of devotion was to

---

58. de Sales, *Introduction to a Devout Life*, 35.

59. Ibid., 40.

60. Ibid., 33.

61. Wright, *A Retreat with Francis de Sales*, 27.

62. Dailey, *Praying with Francis de Sales*, 27.

grow to love God more and more, and friendship had a significant role to play in that process. In spiritual friendship, Francis taught, "a single spirit" united the participants; "holy, sacred," friendships were a "necessary" means for those living in the world to "encourage, assist, and lead one another to perform good deeds."[63] True friends were aware of their mutual affection, and the quality of their communication with each other reflected the quality of their bond. In the *Introduction* he wrote to Philothea:

> The higher the virtues you share and exchange with others, the more perfect your friendship will be. . . . If your mutual and reciprocal exchanges concern charity, devotion, and Christian perfection, O God, how precious this friendship will be! It will be excellent because it comes from God, excellent because it leads to God, excellent because its bond will endure eternally in God.[64]

Francis realized that not every relationship had as its basis virtuous communication or the mutual desire for spiritual growth. A person living the devout life was commanded as a committed Christian to love everyone, and the varied family or social demands of each person's circumstances required different kinds of contacts. The "single spirit" Francis envisioned in spiritual friendships grew in a relationship that was chosen and had as its core an increasing love of God fostered by the exchange of very real human love. To his own cherished friend and spiritual directee St. Jane Frances de Chantal he said this:

> You would not believe how much my heart was strengthened by our resolutions and by everything that contributed to their establishment. I feel an extraordinary sweetness about them as likewise I feel for the love I bear you. Because I love that love incomparably. It is strong, resilient, measureless and unreserved yet gentle, pliant, completely pure and tranquil. In short, if I am not deceived, it is completely in God.[65]

63. de Sales, *Introduction to a Devout Life*, 175.

64. Ibid., 174.

65. Wright, *Bond of Perfection*, 134.

The "honeyed words," "passionate phrases," and "enticing postures" of "vain" friendships were, in Francis' mind, distortions of the kind of God-centered love that unites and ultimately transforms spiritual friends. In the bond of friendship he understood and experienced there was no deficiency of passion or joy, but the deep and genuine human love between devout souls was always "intimately intertwined" with the love of God. It was through the fullness of loving each other that the reality of God's love was most wonderfully encountered, and so Francis could confidently advise that "perfection consists not in having no friendships, but in having only those which are "good, holy, and sacred."[66] These had the "extraordinary sweetness" of love that was incomparable and rested securely and "completely in God."

Francis agreed with St. Teresa of Avila that "particular" friendships were not helpful in a religious community, but he insisted that "people in the world need them to keep safe and assist one another in the many dangerous places they must pass through."[67] He advised that one wishing to live a life of devotion should ask earnestly for a friend after God's own heart as a guide and support, and Francis was certain that God, always caring for the welfare of souls who seek him, would not fail to provide such a friend. It must be a careful choice, Francis counseled, for perhaps "one in ten thousand" would be worthy. Those joined in the bonds of a faithful friendship that was "completely holy, completely sacred, completely divine, completely spiritual,"[68] were signs of God's very presence—real signs that "God, who is love, is indeed alive" in the midst of the world. Four hundred years before *Lumen Gentium*, St. Francis de Sales taught that in the ordinary activities of daily living, holiness was to be found. Outside the enclosures of monasteries and convents, every person was invited to the devout life and to the growth in virtue that was part of its definition. Spiritual friends were gifts given to each other along the way—bright mirrors of the steadfast, overflowing reality of God's eternal love.

66. de Sales, *Introduction to a Devout Life*, 177.
67. Ibid., 176.
68. Ibid., 47.

5

Treasured Earthen Vessels

The psychologist Erich Fromm thought loving was an art. He described mature love as an "active power" that breaks through separateness and isolation to unite one person with another while retaining the integrity of each.[1] This is a process that is always in a state of movement and growth, and it is always a challenge. The communication between two persons in a loving relationship comes from the center of their existence, a core place of aliveness and strength. Out of this center of vital energy flows the prime characteristic of a person who practices the challenging art of loving—the ability to give the other "that which is alive in him . . . his joy . . . his interest . . . his understanding . . . his knowledge . . . his humor . . . his sadness."[2] In this offering, the very self is given, and it is an act of great vitality from one person that brings to birth an echoing response in another. Both people are more alive through such an exchange, Fromm believed, and they both share "in the joy of what they have brought to life."[3] No value can be placed on such a gift that is indeed a treasure, and no sum can balance the worth of loving persons to each other.

1. Fromm, *The Art of Loving*, 20.
2. Ibid., 24.
3. Ibid., 25.

In Christian spirituality, the yearning caused by God's own life deep within us is the source of our vitality, and the gift of our identity given to us through Christ draws us out of ourselves and toward one another. We are called "to direct both our own and others' love together home to God" and the friends with whom we share the spiritual journey are the treasured "earthen vessels" in which we carry the wonder of God's love.[4] St. Therese of Lisieux, St. Elizabeth Ann Seton, and Dorothy Day were women who had the experience of meeting another "from the center of their existence"—from that place of aliveness and strength, which was their core identity in Christ. They were, although in very different circumstances, practitioners of the art of loving who gave the gift of themselves, and in the mutual exchange with their friends, they had the joy of bringing something precious to life.

These were holy women, but they were also fully human persons, "struggling to incarnate the shape of divine life."[5] They lived friendships that were rich and intimate within the context of a deeper reality. Their examples are instructive to those of us still learning to give shape to divine life in our own relationships. A brief summary of their experiences cannot capture the intensity of the "aliveness" that characterized their friendships, but something of their interest, their understanding, and their knowledge can be glimpsed. Erich Fromm wrote that people of every age must face the question of how to "overcome separateness, how to achieve union, how to transcend one's own individual life and find at-onement."[6] The spiritual friendships of these three women are the stories of people who faced that question and integrated their real human love with all the grace of the divine love at work within them.

4. Wright, *A Retreat with Francis de Sales*, 37.

5. Wright, "Reflections on Spiritual Friendship," 27.

6. Fromm, *The Art of Loving*, 9.

ST. THERESE OF LISIEUX AND MAURICE
BELLIERE: CONTEMPLATIVE AND MISSIONARY

"The Lord shall be between you and me . . . forever."

—1 SAM 20:42

In the early evening of September 30, 1897, Therese Martin, twenty-five years old and a Carmelite nun for nine years, died in the infirmary of her convent at Lisieux from tuberculosis. The next day, a French seminarian named Maurice Belliere arrived in Africa to continue his studies for the priesthood and to begin his life as a missionary. Within two weeks he would receive news of Therese's death and understand the reason for the calm and peace he had felt since his arrival. "The saint was near me with her comforting tenderness and strength," he wrote to the prioress at Lisieux, voicing his conviction of Therese's sanctity and his faith in what she herself had once assured him, "I am your sister and your friend, and I will always watch over you."[7]

Maurice and Therese knew each other only through a correspondence of twenty-one letters that lasted less than two years. Maurice was the initiator in 1895 when he wrote to the prioress of the Lisieux Carmel asking that a nun be assigned to pray for his salvation and for his faithfulness to his vocation as a priest. Therese was the nun who was given this assignment and it was one she accepted with joy. She had longed for a brother who was a priest, but the only males born in her family had died in infancy. It seemed to her that in Maurice this long-unrealized dream was to come true. She wrote in her autobiography:

> The unexpected fulfillment of my longing awoke in me
> a joy that I can only call childlike, for I must go back to
> my childhood days to remember pleasure so great. . . . I
> felt as if my soul had been reborn. . . . I understood my

7. Ahern, *St. Therese*, audiocassette.

> new obligations and set to work to fulfill them. I tried
> to increase my fervor and wrote several letters to my
> new brother. It is true that one can help missionaries by
> prayer and sacrifice, but sometimes Jesus chooses to link
> together two souls for His glory and then He lets them
> exchange their thoughts to stir each other to a greater
> love of God.[8]

Under most circumstances, the prioress of a Carmel would not
have allowed the personal correspondence that blossomed between
Therese and Maurice. The advice of Carmel's spiritual mother, St.
Teresa of Avila, concerning the divisive effect of exclusive friendships on the community was well known. Therese, however, was
under the authority of a broad-minded prioress who was also quite
aware of her remarkable spiritual gifts. It was the leniency of this
superior that was directly responsible for the correspondence and
the close relationship that developed between Therese and Maurice as a result. Prayer and sacrifices were part of Therese's vocation
as a Carmelite, but, as she observed, Jesus chose to link these two
souls together in a unique way so that they could "exchange their
thoughts" in their letters and "stir each other to a greater love of
God."[9]

"What we ask of Him is to work for His glory, to love Him
and make Him loved," Therese wrote to Maurice in one of her
first letters to him.[10] They were souls who understood each other
in that common desire. Maurice's ardent aspirations for life as a
missionary priest were deeply sincere but he urgently needed the
prayerful, unwavering support of Therese to compensate for his
lack of confidence. He begged her to continue to send the "beautiful and holy thoughts" that were immensely beneficial to him.[11]
Throughout most of the two years of her correspondence with
Maurice, Therese was in a slow and increasingly agonizing process
of dying from tuberculosis. At the same time, her spirit entered a

8. Therese of Lisieux, *The Story of a Soul*, 144.

9. Ibid.

10. Ahern, *Maurice and Therese*, 83.

11. Ibid., 96.

dark night, which was to last until the moment of her death. As much as Maurice needed Therese to bolster his confidence and to encourage him in his vocation, in her own dark trial, Therese welcomed the opportunity to share with him the basis of the faith to which she clung—her belief in the overwhelming, merciful love of God.

No greatness was required to receive this love. Therese always saw herself as a little soul who could do only little things for God. In her life as a Carmelite, she had come to understand that love was the vocation that held all the others, and her greatest desire was to be God's love and to spread it everywhere. Maurice was her soul's companion who would take that love to the missions where she could not go. As a Carmelite, she would support him with the depth of her prayer and her confidence in the God who loved them both. She wrote to her "dear little brother" just three months before her death, "your letters unite me more closely to God by making me reflect deeply upon the marvels of His mercy and love."[12] Their friendship was grounded solidly in the love of God but they were not hesitant to express their affection for each other in endearing terms. Maurice's grief on learning from Therese of the gravity of her illness was deep and sincere:

> Oh my poor little Sister, what a blow for my poor heart! It was so unprepared. . . . You are about to go away, dear little Sister, and my heart will be alone once more. More than with mother or family it became focused on its sister's love. It found a lovely home in her holy friendship. My heart was happy . . . to feel near it this friendly hand which consoled and strengthened and ennobled it. . . . Oh how it is, how painful for a soul not deeply rooted in God! Nevertheless, His will be done.[13]

Their common devotion to the love of God drew them, in the midst of their real grief and suffering, to turn their attention to the promise of the eternal life in which they both had hope. Therese understood Maurice in all his needs, and she knew the "greatest

12. Ibid., 133.
13. Ibid., 160.

gift she could bestow on him . . . was the assurance of the special place he held in her heart."[14] She poured affection on him as her life came to its end, asking him to "believe that I shall be your *true little* sister for all eternity."[15] Maurice responded that he would have the confidence to expect everything from her, "to count on your help whenever I need it."[16] Jesus was the treasure Maurice found in Therese, and Jesus would continue the link between their souls even after death.

Neither doubted that when Maurice was ordained and began life as a missionary in Africa, Therese would be supporting him with her love and her prayers, not from the Carmel in Lisieux but from heaven. "All that I cannot say to you while I am still here below I shall make you understand from the heights of heaven," she assured him, and it was a promise that sustained Maurice to the end of his own life in 1907.[17] It can be said of Therese that she was "a completely converted Christian who held nothing back for herself."[18] In the generosity and warm affection of the friendship between Therese and Maurice Belliere, the love of God that drew them both linked them together in a holy bond destined to last in him forever.

ST. ELIZABETH ANN SETON AND THE FILICCHI FAMILY: FAMILY FRIENDSHIPS

"Your people shall be my people, and Your God my God."

—RUTH 1:16

14. Ibid., 175.
15. Ibid., 169.
16. Ibid., 199.
17. Ibid., 130.
18. Ibid., 157.

The facts of Elizabeth Ann Seton's life have been well documented in a variety of sources, especially in the thirty-eight years since she became the first American-born canonized saint of the Catholic Church. She herself is responsible for a great deal of material for that documentation, because she left as part of her legacy a large, lively, and articulate body of letters written to a variety of people. It is in her correspondence that the vivid contours of her personality take shape around the framework of the events of her life. One biographer has described that personality as having the qualities of "charity, kindness, patience and long-suffering, plus a natural common sense, wit and breeding" in a combination that captivated everyone she met.[19] The ability to captivate those who knew her blessed Elizabeth with friends throughout her difficult and demanding life, and both her passionate humanity and her commitment to God were reflected in the loving devotion she returned to them.

Throughout the many shifts her life took—widowhood, poverty, single parenthood, conversion to Catholicism, social ostracism, dedication to a religious vocation, the deaths of so many she held dear—friendship was for Elizabeth "a sort of sacrament," it was "her delight, her support," and it was "temperamentally necessary to her."[20] Her friends were her sources of comfort as well as her trusted confidants and advisors, and they were essential players in a life the church has identified as a model for holiness. They were also Elizabeth's teachers, because in her varied interactions with them, she learned to perfect the art of friendship in herself. Among those who were graced to know her, the members of the Filicchi family, particularly Antonio Filicchi, stand out as especially significant. The company of these people at the crucial time of Elizabeth's widowhood opened the doors for her to Catholicism and subsequently to a way of life she could not have imagined.

After the death of Elizabeth's husband in Italy in 1803, she and her young daughter were assisted by the generosity of the Filicchi brothers who had been her husband's business associates.

19. Dirvin, *Mrs. Seton*, 129.
20. Ibid., 54.

They recognized in her a woman of exceptional qualities of both heart and soul, and in whom devotion to God was extraordinarily strong, long before she became a Catholic. When there were a series of delays in her departure for New York, Elizabeth was able to observe in her close association with the Filicchis the depth of their own devotion to God in a faith that, until that time, had been foreign to her as a member of the Episcopal Church. Filippo Filicchi seriously challenged her to recognize her obligation to pray and inquire about Catholicism. With Anabilia Filicchi, Antonio's wife, she visited magnificent Italian churches and from her she learned of the Catholic doctrine of Christ's Real Presence in the Eucharist. At the Mass where Anabilia explained this to her, Elizabeth "put her face in her hands and cried,"[21] and she later wrote to her sister-in-law Rebecca of the profound effect this concept had on her spirit:

> How happy could we be, if we believed what these dear souls believe: that they possess God in the Sacrament, and that He remains in their churches and is carried to them when they are sick!
>
> The other day, in a moment of excessive distress, I fell on my knees without thinking when the Blessed Sacrament passed by, and cried in an agony to God to *bless me*, if He was *there*—that my soul desired only Him.[22]

The intensity of Elizabeth's desire for union with God would be the motivating force in the difficult and painful pathway to conversion that was before her. Throughout much of that time, Antonio Filicchi was the trusted and much-loved friend who assisted her in her study. He both challenged and encouraged her and gave her the affectionate yet realistic support she needed in her difficult circumstances. They loved each other deeply and remained friends until Elizabeth died in 1821. However, it was also a friendship they both needed to understand within the boundaries of each other's life commitments. A relationship of the depth and intensity of this kind that existed between Elizabeth and Antonio requires skill and

21. Ibid., 135.
22. Ibid., 137.

maturity. Each partner must know what they want and understand clearly where the primary commitment of each lies. Elizabeth and Antonio had separate lives that needed to be honored, but they had a common spiritual commitment that gave grace to what she called their "very sincere and uncommon affection."[23] Their friendship was "prudently guarded," and it was Elizabeth's ardent soul that was "constantly immersing their affection in the Heart of God."[24] This portion of a letter written to Antonio came from her depths:

> I would cry out now, as my poor Seton used to: "Antonio, Antonio, Antonio;" but call back the thought, and my soul cries out: "Jesus, Jesus, Jesus!" There it finds rest and heavenly peace. . . . Jonathan loved David as his own soul, and if I was your brother, Antonio, I would never leave you for one hour. But as it is, I try rather to turn every affection to God, well knowing that there alone their utmost exercise cannot be misapplied, and most ardent hopes can never be disappointed.[25]

The sincerity of such a real human love inextricably bound with the divine made Elizabeth's friendship with Antonio—and with each of the Filicchis—permanent. Her gratitude to them for their many kindnesses and for their instrumentality in her conversion never diminished. She depended on their caring and the blessing of their prayers, and Elizabeth, who regarded friendship as "a sort of sacrament" repaid them with a loyal devotion that endured to the end. Before she died, she was still assuring Antonio that "the love of my heart can never grow cold to you and your dear family while it has a beat of life."[26] "I meet you the day of judgement," Filippo had said to her in 1804 when he left her in Italy, already confident that she would choose Catholicism, and that the people of his faith would be her people, and the God his family worshipped would become hers as well. With the Filicchis, and particularly with An-

---

23. Marie Celeste, *The Intimate Friendships*, 73.

24. Dirvin, *Mrs. Seton*, 160–61.

25. Ibid., 161.

26. Marie Celeste, *The Intimate Friendships*, 89.

tonio, she knew love that was "planted, watered, and brought to perfect bloom by God," and that was indeed a gift well received by a vibrant woman who sought to "turn every affection" to him.[27]

DOROTHY DAY AND PETER MAURIN: LOVERS OF THE POOR: "BUILDING A SOCIETY TOGETHER WHERE IT WAS EASIER FOR PEOPLE TO BE GOOD."

"It was not you who chose me, but I who chose you and appointed you to go and bear fruit that will remain."

—JOHN 15:16

The relationship of Dorothy Day and her mentor Peter Maurin, cofounders of the Catholic Worker Movement, was somewhat different from the friendships seen in the lives of St. Therese of Lisieux and St. Elizabeth Ann Seton. The affectionate bonding that existed between those women and their friends, expressed so plainly in the language of their letters, had a different cast in the friendship between Dorothy and Peter. In her book, *Loaves and Fishes*, Dorothy admitted that there were times when she wondered if she really liked Peter. He was an older French peasant with a heavy accent that made listening to him difficult. Furthermore, he was indifferent to the music and literature that Dorothy loved, and he had a mind that knew only one track. Yet at the same time, she acknowledged that, like others in the Movement, she "loved him dearly" and "revered him as a saint."[28] He was for her the friend and teacher who gave her "principles to live by and lessons

27. Dirvin, *Mrs. Seton*, 161.
28. Day, *Loaves and Fishes*, 95.

to study," and a way of life from which she never departed after she met him.[29]

Their first meeting took place in the early 1930s. Dorothy had gone to Washington DC as a reporter for a Catholic magazine to cover a workers' march. The experience of watching the vast numbers of the unemployed jolted her conscience. She felt sharply that her recent conversion to Catholicism had not yet taken on the passionate activism of her earlier life. Before leaving the city, she went to the Basilica of the Immaculate Conception to pray for the marchers and for herself, a prayer she later said "came with tears and with anguish."[30]

> I felt keenly that God was more on the side of the hungry, the ragged, the unemployed, than on the side of the comfortable churchgoers who gave so little heed to the misery of the needy and the groaning of the poor. I . . . prayed that some way would open up for me to do something, to line myself up on their side, to work for them, so that I would no longer feel that I had been false to them in embracing my new-found faith.[31]

When Dorothy arrived back in New York, she found Peter waiting to meet her. He had read some of her writing and was convinced she was the person to help him in his work of addressing the inequities of society from the perspective of faith. He looked like the working man he was, but he was also a person well read in social issues and in the historical and intellectual tradition of the Catholic Church. He began eagerly and immediately to teach Dorothy what she needed to learn to begin to see, as he did, the possibility of building "a society in which it is easier for people to be good."[32] The appearance of this unusual man on her doorstep was for Dorothy the answer to her earnest prayer in Washington. Her conscience and her faith were about to be united to her work, and many years later she commented that meeting Peter Maurin

---

29. Ibid., 104.

30. Day, *The Long Loneliness*, 166.

31. Day, *Loaves and Fishes*, 13.

32. Day, *The Long Loneliness*, 170.

"changed everything, everything. . . . I had finally found a purpose in my life and the teacher I needed."[33]

The program Peter envisioned was ambitious, but it was grounded in the realities of the Great Depression. A society where people were "good" had three components: 1) discussion for the clarification of ideas; 2) the creation of houses of hospitality to welcome the needy; 3) and, the establishment of farming communes to provide shelter, work, and food. Dorothy's journalistic skills would be used in publishing a newspaper to spread the ideas of Peter's program to the common people. By 1935, all of these pieces had their first implementation, and all of her life Dorothy believed that the Catholic Worker Movement would not have been started without Peter Maurin. She was impatient with those who insisted that he was only an "energizer"; to such "condescension" and "incorrect" thinking, she would respond that he was "a leader, a moral leader looking for some people who would link arms with him."[34] She believed he was her spiritual leader as well, a guide who "enabled her idealism to be implemented in daily life through her various involvements with others."[35]

Peter gave Dorothy a sense of the possible, of what could be accomplished by people whose hearts and minds were changed so that "they would observe the new commandment of love" or at least have that desire.[36] She remembered that he told her often they were "long for Jesus" and needed to forget themselves and encourage others to do likewise. It was not the self that was the main concern, he taught Dorothy, but the other; he knew the "surest way to find God, to find the good, was through one's brothers."[37] In Peter's vision of society, people could produce and share sufficiently what was needed for the physical necessities, and they would then have the opportunity to develop their capacities for all that was best in them. This depended on change and an openness to the

33. Coles, *Dorothy Day*, 73.
34. Coles, "Moral Leadership," 9.
35. Ibid., 13.
36. Day, *The Long Loneliness*, 171.
37. Ibid.

"art of human contacts;" spiritually, "it was seeing Christ in others, loving the Christ you saw in others."[38] More importantly, in the gritty reality or in the dull sameness of everyday life, "it was having faith in the Christ in others without being able to see Him—to be blessed in believing without seeing."[39]

Dorothy outlived Peter by thirty years, and it became her task to teach others as he had taught her. She never wavered in her dedication to the Catholic Worker Movement, and she remained convinced of the rightness of that decision because she knew she had not chosen this work by herself. She and Peter had been chosen for each other to live out the charity and friendship that flowed from God and to do it totally in the midst of the daily life they knew. In their devotion to generosity, fairness, and communion, the "good" Peter spoke about became easier to see and to be understood as a possibility for anyone willing to walk a similar path. Peter had the happiness of finding his vocation in life and being certain of it, and with his friend Dorothy, he joined with others "willing to undertake their task in life, striving not only to love God and their brother, but to *show* that love."[40] To the end of her life, Dorothy maintained that without Peter, she would never have found a way of working that "satisfied" her conscience. She became the servant she was because she was blessed with the unusual friendship "of someone with whom she walked in tandem, and whom she regarded as a master teacher—or rather, an emissary of the Master of all of us."[41]

38. Ibid.
39. Ibid.
40. Day, *Loaves and Fishes*, 10.
41. Coles, "Moral Leadership," 14.

6

Fifteen Contemporary
Lessons on Friendship

"Friendship is a sheltering tree."
—SAMUEL TAYLOR COLERIDGE (1772–1834)

Sometimes in life, we get a chance to go back and re-kindle a friendship that was very important to us at one time. That is what happened to Mitch Albom, the author of *Tuesdays with Morrie*. Morrie Schwartz had been Mitch's college professor, mentor, and friend, twenty years prior to publication. In the last months of Morrie's life they reconnected. Knowing that he was dying from Lou Gehrig's disease or amyotrophic lateral sclerosis, Mitch visited Morrie in his study every Tuesday, just as they used to do back in college. Their rekindled friendship turned into one final "class": lessons in how to live.

At one point in their story, Ted Koppel, a TV personality, came to interview Morrie. It was then becoming more difficult for Morrie to speak. Morrie told Koppel about a friend of his, Maurie

Stein, who had taught with Morrie at Brandeis University since the early sixties, and was going deaf. Koppel imagined the two men together one day, one unable to speak, the other unable to hear. "What would that be like, Morrie" he asked? "We will hold hands." Morrie said. "And there'll be a lot of love passing between us. Ted, we've had thirty-five years of friendship. You don't need speech or hearing to feel that."[1]

Having this kind of history with a friend is something we all long for. It's what true friendship is all about. Some people are fortunate enough to develop these kinds of relationships, while others appear to fall short of attaining this goal. But this is where we can learn from the masters. From their lives and their wisdom, we can learn how to appreciate the value of our friends as the "great grace" that friendship is and how to cultivate our own true and lasting friendships. Here are fifteen lessons and stories that have been helpful to me.

1. FRIENDSHIP: A SHELTERING TREE

Samuel Taylor Coleridge said friendship is a sheltering tree. Each one of us needs a sheltering tree—a place we can go to find rest and comfort, a place we feel comfortable sharing our sadness amid the harshness of the realities of life.

Teresa of Avila understood this very well. She said a friend was like a "shield" for one another where each person could find support against the temptations of life and the criticism of others. Also, the friendship of the Filicchi family was certainly a sheltering tree—a major source of comfort for Elizabeth Ann Seton as she tried to find her way in life after the death of her husband at a young age. Their friendship allowed her to have the freedom to sort out the issues confronting her and her young daughter and to find the courage to face the future. Similarly, Therese of Lisieux was a great source of comfort to Maurice Belliere as he departed his homeland for the missions in Africa. Knowing that she would

1. Albom, *Tuesdays with Morrie*, 70–71.

always be there for him was like a sheltering tree—a great source of comfort and encouragement.

Sometimes, groups can also be sheltering trees for us. Hospice, for example, is often this for people who are dying as well as their families. At a very important and vulnerable time, hospice volunteers bring peace and comfort on a person's final journey. Another organization, Compassionate Friends, was clearly a sheltering tree for my wife and me when our son was stillborn some years ago. Filled with sorrow and grief, these people provided a safe place to grieve. They gave us the freedom to feel all the emotions that accompany this kind of loss and set us on a path to healing.

2. FRIENDS: HELP US FIND WHOLENESS

When I first met Kathy, her psychology practice was barely surviving. She shared offices with a group of physicians, and, desperate to be accepted and work under what she perceived as the umbrella of their credibility, she took whatever crumbs fell from their professional table. Hers was the smallest office in the complex and hers was the only name not listed on the office door. It was obvious from the beginning how dedicated and gifted a therapist she was. However, this compromising attitude troubled me, although I didn't say anything about it at the time. But Kathy felt validated by the association and she was convinced that she needed referrals from the doctors in order to have patients.

Kathy was a shy person, a little apologetic and sometimes hesitant in trying to find the right words in a conversation. She was also just the slightest bit clumsy. However, all this actually made her very endearing. You felt somehow at home with her and safe. Her patients loved her.

One day she told me she was moving from her present office. Although I was pleased, I asked her why she had decided to leave. "They don't have wheelchair access," she said. I guess I looked surprised so she went on to say that she had not told me everything about herself. She continued to tell her story and said that years ago when she was young, she had a very serious stroke and was not expected to recover. "I was astonished," I said. "I had no idea." She replied, "nobody does." I went on to ask her why she had kept this part of her life a secret. Almost in tears, she said that for years she had felt damaged and ashamed. "I wanted to put it behind me," she said. "I thought if I could be seen as normal I would be more than I was." And so she had guarded her secret closely. Neither her colleagues nor her patients knew. She had felt certain that others would not refer to her or want to come to her for help if they knew. However, now she was no longer sure this was true.

"So, what do you plan to do now?" I asked her. She looked down at her hands in her lap. "I think I will just be myself," she told me. "I will see people like myself. People who are not like others. People who have had strokes and other brain injuries. People who can never be normal again. I think I can help them be whole." Over the past five years, Kathy has become widely known for her work. She has been honored by several community groups and interviewed in newspapers. She often speaks on these kinds of topics and consults for businesses and hospitals. The many people she has helped refer others to her. Her practice is thriving. Her own name is on the door. All Kathy needed in order to be whole was the courage of her own vulnerability.

Maurice Belliere wanted to be a missionary in Africa but lacked confidence in his talents and abilities. However, his correspondence with Therese of Lisieux enabled him to find the confidence he needed to be successful in his ministry. Similarly, after Elizabeth Ann Seton's husband died, the Filicchis allowed her to be weak, confused and afraid, so she could gradually become strong and discover what God wanted of her.

Friends help each other face their own vulnerabilities and help turn them into strengths. They help us learn to accept our woundedness in life and in the process help us find wholeness.

3. FRIENDS: ALLOW US TO KNOW WE ARE "GOOD ENOUGH"

In John Steinbeck's splendid novel *East of Eden*, there is a scene in which a son gives his father a present that he has selected with great care and for which he has sacrificed a great deal. The father spurns it. The reader understands that the father does this because he is an emotionally wounded person who has trouble seeing his son's better qualities and also has difficulty believing that he himself deserves a special present. But the boy, lacking the reader's perspective, cannot understand that. The message he gets is he is not good enough, and that rejection will color the rest of his life.

There are a lot of people in the world walking around feeling like they are not good enough, feeling disappointed in who they are and not believing they deserve to be loved. There can also be something in the human soul that causes us to think less of ourselves every time we do something wrong. It may be the result of parents who expected too much of us, or maybe teachers who took for granted what we did right and focused instead on everything we got wrong. And sometimes, it may be good for us to feel that way. It may make us more sensitive to what we do wrong and move us to repent and grow. But it may also lead to our setting unrealistically high standards for ourselves and for others.

So often we feel we need to be perfect for people to love us and that somehow we forfeit that love if we ever fall short of perfection. There are few emotions more capable of leaving us feeling bad about ourselves than the conviction that we don't deserve to be loved. But God doesn't stop loving us every time we do something wrong, and neither should we stop loving ourselves and each other for being less than perfect.

Several years ago, Rabbi Harold Kushner wrote a book titled *How Good Do We Have to Be?* In this work, Kushner emphasizes the fact that no one is perfect. Yet many people measure themselves and others against impossibly high standards. But the result is always the same—guilt, anger, depression, and disappointment. A healthier approach, Kushner maintains, is to learn how to put our human shortcomings into proper perspective. We need to learn how to accept ourselves and others even when we and they are less than perfect.[2]

In over thirty years as a psychotherapist, I have learned a number of things about perfectionism: 1) perfectionism, is found, in varying degrees, in most people. We twist ourselves in knots, doing things to gain approval and love. It would be much healthier if we could let go of what people think and accept ourselves, warts and all. 2) The quest for perfection is exhausting. We need to be gentle and compassionate with ourselves, particularly when we make mistakes. No one is perfect. We need to stop holding ourselves to ridiculously high standards in a quest to prove our worth to others. We are already enough. Compassion towards ourselves leads to compassion towards others. 3) Having the courage to let others "see who we really are" can be very healing. When we are our authentic selves, we wind up connecting with others on a deeper level. Don't we love the company of people who are "real" and comfortable in their own skin?

These are the issues a friend can help us understand. Sir Thomas Browne said "we carry within us, the wonders we seek without us." Like God, a friend helps us understand we are good enough the way we are, that we don't have to be perfect for our friend to love us. Like Aelred of Rievaulx, who saw a friend as a kindred spirit and another self, like Teresa of Avila who saw a friend as a shield for one another, like Thomas Aquinas who saw a friend as a treasured companion and a marvelous gift, they knew friends are wonderful graces God gives us to know we are lovable even with our faults, sinfulness, and imperfections. Sometimes, simply being accepted as we are and cared about by another can affect a person in very profound ways.

2. Kushner, *How Good Do We Have to Be?*, 4.

4. FRIENDSHIPS: SOMETIMES DEVELOP BETWEEN VERY DIFFERENT KINDS OF PEOPLE AND IN THE STRANGEST PLACES

In 1932, Dorothy Day traveled to Washington DC to join in a march for the unemployed. It was during the Great Depression. After the march, she went to the Basilica of the Immaculate Conception to pray for guidance as to how she could continue to live out the values she had discovered there in wanting to work with the poor. When she returned to New York, she was met by Peter Maurin, who was also looking for someone to help him with his ideas of building a better society.

Dorothy and Peter were very different personalities. In fact, Dorothy wasn't even sure she liked Peter in the beginning. She called him a "character." But they were both open to the working of God in their lives to help each other serve the poor. Sometimes, this is the way friendships develop. We must always remain open to this grace of friendship because it can lead to very important paths of growth in our lives.

Similarly, as a cloistered Carmelite nun, Therese of Lisieux would never have expected to become friends with Maurice Belliere, a missionary priest in Africa. Although they actually never met each other in person, their friendship grew through their correspondence. They became great friends and were open to the grace of God to serve the church in very different ways.

When Maisie Ward was waiting to meet Caryll Houselander outside the door of her apartment, she certainly was not expecting to meet someone about whom she would later write, "we felt the perfect ease of long intimacy, and began a conversation to be picked up at any moment thereafter."[3] And Thomas Merton, a cloistered Cistercian monk, was certainly not expecting to have what he called one of the greatest graces of his life in downtown Louisville, Kentucky where he experienced "a oneness with all these people," which had a profound impact on his life.

---

3. Ward, *Caryll Houselander*, 206.

Joan was a librarian who would soon be forty. She had always lived alone. Charitably speaking, Joan could be described as very, very plain. However, her sisters and her mother were truly beautiful women. When you looked at her, you could tell her clothes were not very becoming to her. She wore no jewelry or make-up and her hair was pulled back with a rubber band into a ponytail. Her finest feature was her eyes. Clear and gray, they were now filled with tears.

Life is not easy for a plain woman. From early childhood, she had felt ashamed of her looks and was painfully shy. The response of others to her simply confirmed her sense of wrongness. In school, children had made fun of her appearance. As a teenager, her peers had avoided her. Her family, while loyal, were often apologetic about the way she looked. Many years before, she had simply given up. In her entire life she had never had an intimate relationship. She felt at ease only in her home or in the library. "Librarians are invisible," she told me. She spent days at work and her evenings in front of the TV. She had lived this way for a long time.

As her fortieth birthday grew closer, Joan became more depressed. I worried about her and began to see her more often. I offered her a place of acceptance and caring, but in the end it was not me, but my patients, who healed her.

As she sat in my waiting room, week after week, she began to respond to the others she saw there. Many of them were hurting like she was. She had never met people like them before, and she was surprised that she felt so comfortable with them. Although she was shy, she eventually began to speak with some of them. She had also noticed that other people often came with these patients, people who drove or shopped or helped in a variety of ways. After thinking about this for a while, she hesitantly told me that if some of my patients had no one or if their families needed an extra hand, she would be glad to help.

This was how Joan met Bill. He was a handsome thirty-two year old man who had become HIV positive about a year after his partner was diagnosed with AIDS. Bill had nursed him through his long, progressive illness and ultimate death. Slowly, he too became sick and needed help.

At first, Joan drove Bill to doctors' appointments much as she drove several others. However, most of the others had some family, but Bill was alone. As time went on, she began to shop for him and then to cook extra food at home, freeze it, and take it to him for dinner. They became friends. As things became worse, his parents had flown in to see him several times. They were older now and it had been hard for them at first, but they were a close family and had been able to support Bill in ways that really mattered. Joan had met them too, and liked them. Like Bill, they were kind people.

Within a year, Bill became very ill. His parents had wanted him to come home but he had lived in California for many years and wanted to stay there. He had applied for hospice care but discovered he was not eligible because there was no one living with him who could act as his caregiver. Many of his closest friends had already died and he had no one to turn to for help. After much prayer and reflection, Joan moved in.

Bill died in the spring. When I heard the news I called Joan because I was concerned about her and wondered if she would be able to handle things. Her depression had lifted somewhat over the past several months, but I knew that Bill's death would be a great blow to her.

A few weeks later, she came to see me and told me she had been visiting Bill's parents and had attended his funeral. As she talked about the events that had led to his death, I noticed that she was wearing lipstick. When I commented on this, she looked away from me and seemed to blush. Continuing with her story, she told me about something that had happened shortly before Bill died. He had been very weak and mostly bedridden for some time. One morning he had not been doing well, and so she called him from the library several times during the day. The hospice social worker and the nurse visited him daily and often a neighbor would look in, but as the day went on she worried about his being at home alone until she finished work.

Coming home, she had run up the stairs, her arms full of groceries. She opened the door, calling his name loudly so that he could hear her in his bedroom. But Bill was not in his bedroom. Fully dressed in a jacket, shirt, and tie, he was sitting in the living room waiting for her. His clothes, still elegant, looked as if they had been bought for a much larger man, but his hair was carefully combed and he had shaved. The effort involved was hard for her to even imagine.

Stunned, she asked him why he had gotten dressed. He had looked at her for a long moment. Then, he eased off the couch, and, getting down on one knee, he had asked her to marry him. She had put the groceries down then and helped him up. Hugging him for the first time, she told him how very important he was to her.

I looked at her in silence. Still blushing, she met my eye. "In my heart I did marry him you know," she told me. "He will be here with me always."[4]

What we see in each of these experiences is the importance of being open to friendships in life that can develop between different kinds of people, in the strangest places, and when we least expect it. If we can remain open, then we can experience what C. S. Lewis said: "friends are not chance acquaintances but gifts given to us by God."

5. FRIENDSHIPS: DO BETTER WHEN FOCUSED ON SOMEONE OR SOMETHING ELSE OUTSIDE OF THEMSELVES

There can be a danger in friendships that occurs when friends become too focused on each other. A colleague of mine once termed this concern "navel gazing" or "belly button staring." This often happens when friendships first begin. There is a natural excitement to new friendships in which people are first getting to know each other. However, after a period of time when the "newness"

4. Remen, *My Grandfather's Blessings*, 293–96.

wears off, friendships require a significant amount of effort if they are to mature and endure. In other words, there are a lot of "ups" and "downs" with genuine friendships.

Perhaps this is why so many wise people as well as the saints knew that for friends to grow and mature, they need to be focused on someone or something outside of themselves. Both classical and Christian writers emphasize this insight. Aristotle and Cicero believed that striving for virtue was the important ingredient. Aristotle felt it was in association with a virtuous friend that one grows in virtue. He thought friends should be sources of virtue and not objects of completion. Cicero also believed friendship was based on the common pursuit of virtue and not financial profit, flattery, or sensuality.

Among numerous Christian writers, St. Jerome felt that Jesus was to be the "cement" in a relationship. As this centering aspect of a friendship developed, he believed the natural feelings friends have for each other would be sublimated in a healthy way into their ministries. This "outside focus" would help friends to always orient their friendships into growthful patterns.

St. Aelred of Rievaulx and St. Teresa of Avila both emphasized that the major role of friends was to help each other grow in the spiritual life. By maintaining this perspective, friends then would be able to grow in their love of God and each other. Moreover, St. Thomas Aquinas saw friendship as the extension and expression of the depth of our friendship with God.

It is also important to understand that even though St. Therese of Lisieux and Maurice Belliere never saw each other in person, they were able to become close friends because Christ was the glue of their relationship. What the masters understood was that when Jesus was the "cement" of the relationship, then friends would be open to the graces of the relationship and to see, like St. Elizabeth Ann Seton, that friends were a "sort of sacrament." In this way, friends were more likely to be open to become instruments of the Lord in their everyday lives.

This idea was equally true for Dorothy Day and Peter Maurin. What kept them connected at a very deep level was their love of God and their love and service to the poor. Their common and constant desire to make the world a better place where "it is easier for people to be good" kept the focus of their friendship outside of themselves and enabled them to be of service to others. And even though their personalities were very different, Dorothy always felt that Peter gave her what she called a "sense of the possible" as well as a real plan on how to achieve their common goals. This solidified their friendship over the years and allowed them to minister to the poor through the ups and downs of life.

6. FRIENDS: HELP US LIVE WITH MYSTERY

One of my favorite quotes is from the writing of Rainer Maria Rilke. He says,

> I beg you . . . to be patient toward all that is unsolved in your heart and try to love the *questions themselves* like locked rooms and like books that are written in a very foreign tongue. Do not seek the answers, which cannot be given you because you would not be able to live them. And the point is, to live everything. *Live* the question now. Perhaps you will then gradually, without noticing it, live along some distant day into the answer.[5]

By its very nature, mystery cannot be solved, can never be known. Many of us have not been raised to cultivate a sense of mystery. In our society, it is particularly difficult to live with our questions. We are trained to answer questions. We pride ourselves in solving the unknown. We like things fixed, figured out, and nailed down. I once saw a poster on a wall with these words attributed to the eminent family therapist Virginia Satir: "Most people prefer the certainty of misery to the misery of uncertainty." Some people even see our inability to solve the unknown as an insult to our competence, almost a personal failing. Seen in this way, the unknown becomes a call to action. But mystery does not require action; it requires our attention. Mystery requires that we listen

5. Rilke, *Letters to a Young Poet*, 35.

and become open. When we meet with the unknown in this way, we can be touched by a wisdom that can transform our lives.

Jesus was a master at using questions to invite people to grow. "What are you looking for?" "Who do you say that I am?" "Do you want to get well?" "Why do you not understand what I say?" "Do you love me?" The New Testament is full of questions.

There is an art to living your questions. You peel them. You listen to them. You let them spawn new questions. You hold the unknowing inside. You linger with it instead of rushing into half-baked answers. Jesuit priest and writer Anthony de Mello put it very well: "Some people will never learn anything because they grasp too soon. Wisdom, after all, is not a station you arrive at, but a manner of traveling. . . . To know exactly where you are headed may be the best way to go astray. Not all who loiter are lost."[6]

As a matter of fact, those who "loiter" in the question long enough will "live into" the answer. "Seek and you will find," Jesus said (Matt 7:7). I sometimes wonder if this means "seek *long enough* and you will find." It is the patient act of dwelling in the darkness of a question that eventually unravels the answer.

Therese of Lisieux and Maurice Belliere, Elizabeth Ann Seton and the Filicchi family as well as Dorothy Day and Peter Maurin helped each other live with mystery and live into the unknown. And there were so many questions, so many unknown dimensions occurring in their lives that not only did they trust that God was leading them through each other but they believed that gradually the mystery, the unknown would be made clear. Their friendships encouraged them to listen and become open so that their lives could be touched by wisdom. And through this process, their lives were transformed.

Everything and everyone possesses a dimension of the unknown. Mystery helps us to see ourselves and others from the largest possible perspective. To be living is to be unfinished. Nothing and no one is complete. The world and everything in it is *alive*. Even as a nation, if we lose our sense of mystery, we can become a nation of burned out people. People who wonder do not burn out.

6. de Mello, *The Heart of the Enlightened*, 38.

A sense of mystery can take us beyond disappointment and judgment to a place of expectancy. It opens in us an attitude of listening and respect. This is what friends do for each other. A fellow questioner helps us learn how to *live* our questions instead of suppressing them. Emily Dickinson once wrote: "I dwell in possibility." If everyone has in them the dimension of the unknown, possibility is present at all times. Wisdom then is possible at all times.

Mystery requires that we relinquish an endless search for answers and "learn to love the questions themselves." It requires a willingness to not understand everything at times. Perhaps real wisdom lies in not seeking answers at all. After all these years, I have begun to wonder if the secret of living well is not in having all the answers but in pursuing unanswerable questions in the company of good friends.

7. FRIENDS: VALIDATE OUR WORTH AS A HUMAN BEING

The friendship and dedication of Dorothy Day and Peter Maurin to serve the poor was extraordinary. Ministering to them through the Great Depression required a steadfastness that most of us can only imagine. But the ability to encourage one another in their darkest hours allowed them to care for the poor for over forty years. Besides providing tangible things for them like food, clothing, and shelter, what they did at a deeper level was to validate their worth as persons. Hopefully, this was the more lasting gift.

After a dozen years, Alzheimer's disease had virtually destroyed Linda's brain, erasing her memories and with them all of her sense of who she was. Confined to a nursing home, she was adrift and frightened, given to pacing back and forth in a seemingly endless fashion filled with a nameless anxiety. Such repetitive pacing is common in people at the last stages of this disease, almost as if they are being driven to search for something hopelessly lost.

All the staff's efforts to ease her fear had failed. For a long time she was at rest only when she slept, and her unending movement had caused her to become painfully thin. Then one day, quite by accident, as she passed the full-length mirror that hung to the left of the door to the courtyard, she caught sight of her own reflection in the glass. Becoming still for the first time in many months, she stood before it, fascinated, an odd expression on her face. She looked as if she had just met a friend from long ago, someone whose face was vaguely familiar but whose connection to oneself cannot be immediately recalled.

As a result of her disease, Linda had not spoken in many months. But drawn to the image in the mirror for reasons long forgotten, she began to speak to it in a language all her own. Day after day she would stand and talk to the woman in the mirror for hours on end. It made her calm.

The nurses welcomed this new behavior with relief. Her endless pacing and anxiety had made her very difficult to care for. Accustomed to much random senseless behavior on the part of their patients, they paid little further attention to how she now spent her time. But her doctor saw this differently. Every day on his rounds, he would stop at the mirror and spend some time with this patient. Standing next to her, he too would talk to the woman in the mirror with his usual kindness and respect. Once at the end of one of his longer chats with Linda's reflection, he was deeply moved to notice Linda had tears in her eyes. The nurses were deeply moved as well. Unable to cure his patient's brutal disease, this true physician instinctively strengthened her last connection to herself with his simple presence and validated her worth as a human being.[7]

For Linda, who saw herself in the mirror, it was like meeting someone she had known a long time ago. Gradually, she was able to speak to herself in the mirror in a language all her own. It was like coming home to herself. This is the way it is with friends. In many spoken and unspoken ways, friends often speak to each other in a language all their own. Maisie Ward said that after she met Caryll Houselander "we both felt the perfect ease of long intimacy, and began a conversation to be picked up at any moment thereafter." This kind of familiarity and intimacy is what true friendship is all about.

7. Remen, *My Grandfather's Blessings*, 103–4.

8. FRIENDS: HELP US LIVE WITH INTEGRITY

After thirty years of working as a psychotherapist with people who are in pain, I have come to realize how much stress is caused by the sad fact that many of us believe in one way and live in quite another. Stress may be more a matter of personal integrity than time pressure, determined by the distance between our authentic values and how we live our lives.

This may explain why some people in the face of what one might imagine is the most overwhelming stress, life-threatening illness, notice their stress level has actually diminished and they feel more joy. Certainly their illness causes them concern, worry, and often fear; yet they often report that their lives are less stressful now than when they were well. Such people seem to have found through their suffering a deep sense of what is most important to them, and the courage to bring their lives into alignment with it for the first time. Rather than using their strength to endure situations and relationships that betray their deepest values, they have used their strength to make needed changes in their lives.

In the midst of her treatment, one client with breast cancer told me how surprised she was to notice this change in her stress level. "For the first time I am sailing my boat by my own star. My God, have I sailed it by everything else! And allowed everyone else to take a turn at the tiller. All my life I've headed against myself, against my own direction. But now I have a deep sense of my way, and I am loyal to it. This is my boat and it was made to sail in this direction, by this star. You asked why I seem so much more peaceful now? Well, I am living all in one piece."

Each of us has this kind of star. It is called the soul. Unfortunately, it is often easier to see it and follow it after it has grown dark.

Perhaps the root cause of stress is not simply overbearing bosses, long commutes, ill-behaved children, or the breakdown of relationships. It is the loss of a sense of our soul. If so, all the ways in which we have attempted to ease stress cannot heal it at the deepest level. Stress may heal only through the recognition that we cannot betray our spiritual nature without paying a great price. It is not that we have a soul but that we are a soul.

There are many practices that can awaken us and deepen our sense of the soul, among them prayer, meditation, fasting, and ritual. One of the most surprising of these is the experience of great loss. I have learned much about the power of the soul from people who have lost almost everything they once thought was important.

The soul is not an idea or a belief; it is an experience. It may awaken in us through dreams, music, art, work, parenthood, or our friends. Sometimes, it will come for seemingly no reason at all. It overtakes us at times in the midst of daily life. Spiritual experience is not taught; it is found, uncovered, discovered, recovered. These sorts of experiences are common. They happen to all of us, sophisticated and unsophisticated, educated and uneducated, often when least expected. Many people discount them or devalue them or simply barely notice them. Yet they can change lives.

Friends help us live with integrity. They help us "sail our own boat" in our own direction and follow our own star. Therese of Lisieux certainly did that for Maurice Belliere. Her friendship gave him courage and strength to follow his own star as a missionary in Africa. Dorothy Day and Peter Maurin also did this for each other. They helped each other live with integrity and be true to their authentic selves as they pursued their ideals of living with and serving the poor. Even though they had to face much opposition in their efforts, it was the strength of their friendship that supported both of them. Similarly, it was the friendship of Elizabeth Ann Seton and the Filicchi family that encouraged Elizabeth to discover the Catholic faith, which became the bedrock of her life. And when it came time for Elizabeth to leave them and come to America to face the unknown, it was the strength of their friendship that allowed her to be true to herself and follow her own star.

9. FRIENDS: "CLOTHE US WITH RESPECT"

In Robert Coles' account of meeting Dorothy Day, he recalled that Dorothy was sitting at a table talking with a woman who was obviously drunk. At first, Coles thought this was very strange—that she would be wasting her time trying to talk with a woman who could hardly speak coherently. But as he watched her, he could tell that Dorothy was trying to be present to this lady, which left a remarkable impression on him. Even though she was drunk, Dorothy had paid attention to her. She had "noticed her." For that moment at least, Dorothy had clothed her with respect.

A friend is certainly someone in our lives who always notices that we are there. They make us feel we are important, special. They are present to us on good days and bad. And maybe this is what people need in life—to know that they are important and special to someone.

Morrie Schwartz, in *Tuesdays with Morrie,* said he would not have been the man he was without the years he spent working at a mental hospital just outside Washington, DC, a place with the deceptively peaceful name of Chestnut Lodge. It was one of Morrie's first jobs after finishing his master's degree and a PhD from the University of Chicago. Having rejected medicine, law, and business, Morrie had decided the research world would be a place where he could contribute without exploiting others.

Morrie was given a grant to observe mental patients and record their treatments. While the idea seems common today, it was groundbreaking in the early 1950s. Morrie saw patients who would scream all day. Patients who would cry all night. Patients soiling their underwear. Patients refusing to eat, having to be held down, medicated, fed intravenously.

One of the patients, a middle-aged woman, came out of her room every day and lay face down on the tile floor, stayed there for hours, as doctors and nurses stepped around her. No one hardly noticed her and certainly no one paid attention to her. Morrie watched in horror. He took notes, which is what he was there to do. Every day she did the same thing: came out in the morning, lay on the floor, stayed there until the evening, talking to no one, ignored by everyone. It saddened Morrie. He began to sit on the floor with her, even lay down alongside her, trying to draw her out of her misery. Eventually, he got her to sit up, and even return to her room. They were gradually becoming friends. What she mostly wanted, he learned, was the same thing many people want—someone to notice she was there.[8]

Another woman—who would spit at everyone else—took to Morrie and called him her friend. They talked each day, and the staff was at least encouraged that someone had gotten through to her.

Morrie observed that most of the patients there had been rejected and ignored in their lives, made to feel they didn't exist, just like the drunk lady Dorothy spent time with. Having a friend "who notices that we are there" and "clothes us with respect" is a healing grace for everyone in life. To believe we are truly special and important brings a peace that is life-giving.

10. FRIEND: BEING A "LAP" FOR EACH OTHER

In my counseling practice, I have learned that denial, anger, and rationalizations are some of the common ways people deal with suffering. But few of these are places of refuge. Most of these coping mechanisms will disconnect us from the very life we hope to live and can undermine our health in a variety of ways. However, the sad part of this is that we can never hide from suffering. Suffering is a part of being alive. Hiding ourselves means only that we will have to suffer alone.

In the presence of suffering, everyone needs to find a place of refuge. This is what Elizabeth Ann Seton needed when her husband died at such a young age. This was clearly a devastating blow to her. Her loss was beyond words. After this kind of tragedy, she seemed inconsolable. But then she began to associate more with the Filicchi family, with whom she gradually became close friends. This family became a place of refuge for her where she knew she didn't have to suffer alone. These friends in the Filicchi family allowed her to grieve and eventually find her way to the Catholic

8. Albom, *Tuesdays with Morrie*, 109–10.

religion, which gradually opened up new opportunities for her to serve God and other people.

Vicky, a highly skilled AIDS doctor, keeps a picture of her grandmother in her home and sits before it for a few minutes every day before she leaves for work. Her grandmother was an Italian-born woman who held her family very close. She was also a very wise woman. Once when Vicky was very small, her kitten was killed in an accident. It was her first experience of death and she was devastated. Her parents had encouraged her not to be sad, telling her that her kitten was in heaven now with God. Despite these assurances, she had not been comforted. She had prayed to God, asking him to give her kitten back. But God did not respond.

In her sorrow, she turned to her grandmother and asked "Why?" Her grandmother had not told her that her kitten was in heaven like so many other adults had done. Instead, she had simply held her and reminded her of the time when her grandfather had died. She, too, had prayed to God, but God had not brought grandpa back. She did not know why. Vicky laid her head on her grandmother's shoulder and sobbed. When she was finally able to look up, she saw her grandmother was crying as well.

Although her grandmother could not answer her questions, a great sadness had been lifted and she felt able to go on. All the assurances that Peaches was in heaven had not given her this strength or peace. "My grandmother was a lap," Vicky said, "a place of refuge." The doctor knew a great deal about AIDS, but what she really wanted to be for her patients was a lap. A place from which they could face what they had to face and not be alone.

Taking refuge does not mean hiding from life. It means finding a place of strength, the capacity to live the life we have been given with greater courage. Elizabeth Ann Seton found a place of refuge, a lap, with the Filicchi family. And isn't this one of the things our friends do for us? With them, we can find places of refuge, a lap to rest in. Maybe what everyone needs is a lap.

11. FRIENDS: PART OF THE "WHITTLING PROCESS"

Aristotle believed friendship established the possibility of genuine unselfishness in human relationships. He felt friends are loved for themselves—not for their usefulness or pleasure. Similarly, Cicero said friendship was the most important and attractive human bond between people because it was based on the common pursuit of virtue and not on financial profit, flattery, or sensuality. He believed the most satisfying experience a person can have is to have someone you can speak to freely as your own self about any and every subject. When one thinks of a true friend, that person is looking at him or herself in the mirror. Even when a friend is absent, he is present all the same.

There is an old Carolina story I like about a country boy who had a great talent for carving beautiful dogs out of wood. Every day he sat on his porch whittling, letting the shavings fall around him. One day a visitor, greatly impressed, asked him the secret of his art. "I just take a block of wood and whittle off the parts that don't look like a dog," he replied.

In rather simplistic, yet profound language, this story describes the movement of growth each of us is called to. We are invited to gently whittle away the parts of ourselves that don't resemble the true self. However, in "spiritual whittling," we don't simply discard the shavings. Transformation happens not by rejecting these parts of ourselves but by gathering them up and integrating them. Through this process we reach a new wholeness.

Much of this whittling process lies in trying to discover how we are living falsely. Thomas Merton envisioned much of the spiritual life as whittling away the false self in order to become the true self. He called the struggle for authenticity a "contemplative crisis" and insisted that no one can avoid it, that eventually we all "get the treatment." According to Merton, "one's actual self may be far from 'real,' since it may be profoundly alienated from one's own deep spiritual identity. To reach one's 'real self' one must, in fact, be delivered from that illusory and 'false self' whom we have created."[9] Merton believed we are not very good at recognizing illusions, least of all the ones we cherish about ourselves.

One of the ways that friends are the "greatest of all gifts," as Cicero says, is that they are given to us to help us grow in life. They can help us discover the ways we are living falsely and thereby help us to find our true selves. St. Jerome believed a friend is "one half of one's soul" or "another self." He felt that we are able to talk with a friend as a "second self." And because of this ability to share ourselves with a friend, we can come to discover our true selves and live more authentically. In essence, friends help the whittling process in all of us.

One of the reasons St. Teresa of Avila thought that friends were such a grace in life was because she believed friends should be able to correct each other and be less defensive with each other. In other words, hearing a criticism from a friend would allow the other person to "hear" the criticism, knowing it was coming from a loving friend who only wanted his or her good. This then would also become part of the whittling process, allowing the other person to grow in authenticity.

In 1892, Maurice Belliere was a young seminarian on his way to Africa as a missionary. However, he was very fearful about taking this step and clearly lacked confidence in himself. This was the primary reason he wrote to the Mother Superior of the Carmelites to ask for one of the sisters to pray for him. Therese of Lisieux was chosen for this task and thus began a unique friendship in which Maurice could freely share his fears. Because of their correspondence, Therese was able to gradually help him increase his self-esteem and build his confidence. He felt safe and secure in sharing his fears with her. Moreover, St. Aelred of Rievaulx felt that a friend was a person "to whom you need have no fear to confess your failings—someone that you could tell the secrets of your heart." This, too, was so true for Maurice. Because he trusted Therese as a true friend, he could open up about his lack of confidence and she could then advise him.

9. Merton, *The New Man*, 63.

Friends are also great sources of encouragement to each other. In fact, one of the phrases used in the New Testament for encouragement is to "put a new heart into." Clearly, this is what Dorothy Day and Peter Maurin did for each other. They encouraged one another in their ministry of serving the poor. Whenever one of them became discouraged, the other one was there to pick them up—to put a new heart into their friend. And after Elizabeth Ann Seton's husband died at a young age and left her with a young daughter, the members of the Filicchi family were there for her to encourage her in her search. Furthermore, after her search led her to the Catholic Church, they were again there for her when she decided to come to America. Being true friends, they became sources of comfort to her as she embarked on this new journey.

12. FRIENDS: HELP US BECOME THE PERSON WE WERE MEANT TO BE

In Sufi literature, there is a story that goes like this. Once upon a time there was a kingdom of great abundance. The fields grew crops twice the size of normal fruits and vegetables, the cows gave cream instead of milk, and the people were productive and happy. The pride of this kingdom was the young prince, the only child of the king and queen. The hopes of everyone were pinned on this stellar young man, and when he walked in the street the people murmured to one another, "How perfect he is in every way. What a perfect king he will make some day." The prince spent almost all his time studying with those who were teaching him how to be the perfect king.

All went well in the kingdom until one day the prince could not be found. Courtiers searched the palace. "The prince is missing," they said, and people everywhere were in despair. The distraught king and queen ran through the thousand rooms of the palace calling the prince's name. There was no answer. Eventually a little serving maid, sweeping the Great Hall, happened to look under the banquet table and saw the prince there. He was stark naked. "Sire," she gasped in alarm, "what are you doing under there. Where are your clothes?"

"I am a chicken," the prince told her. "I do not need any clothes." Upon hearing this, she ran shrieking to the king and queen, saying that she had found the prince and he had gone mad.

The entire castle gathered in the Hall to see this tragedy for themselves. People tried to persuade the prince to come out from under the table, or even to put on his clothes, but he refused, saying only that he was a chicken. They tried to tempt him out from under the table with the finest of foods, but he would not eat. "I am a chicken," he told them. Eventually the little serving maid scattered a handful of corn under the table, which the prince ate gratefully.

The kingdom was in chaos. The king sent out a call for wise men to come out to heal the prince's madness, and many responded. One by one, they spoke to the prince, trying to convince him that he was not a chicken, and one by one they left defeated. "I am a chicken," the prince told them all.

At last, the supply of wise men was exhausted, and the king did not know where else to turn. One day, an old farm woman asked for an audience with the king. "I will cure your son," she told him. The king looked dubious. "Are you a wise woman?" he asked her. "No," she replied "A scholar?" "No," she said. "Then how will you cure my son?" "I will cure your son because I understand chickens." What is the harm, the king thought. We have tried everything else. And so he commanded a page to show the old woman into the Great Hall.

As soon as she entered the Hall, the old woman removed all her clothes, crept under the table, and sat down next to the prince. The prince looked at her and said nothing. In a little while, a servant came and scattered a few handfuls of corn, and when the prince began to eat, the old woman also pecked at the corn. They sat together in silence for some time longer. Finally the prince said to the old woman, "Who are you?"

"And you?" she replied. "Who are you?"

"I am a chicken," said the prince.

"Ah," said the old woman, "I am a chicken, too."

The prince thought about this for several days. Gradually he began to talk to the old woman about the things that are important to chickens, which are different from the things important to people. She understood as only another chicken could understand. They spoke not about the world as it is but about the world as it could be. They became friends.

After several weeks, the old woman called to one of the serving girls and told her to bring some clothes. When the clothes arrived, she dressed herself. The prince was horrified. "You have betrayed me!" he shouted. "You told me you were a chicken!"

"But I *am* a chicken," said the old woman. "I can wear clothes and still be a chicken." The prince thought about this for some time. Then he turned to the pile of clothing and dressed himself also. They continued their conversations as before and continued to eat corn together.

After a few days more, the old woman called to one of the serving girls and told her to bring a fine meal and set it on the table. When the meal arrived, she crawled out from under the table and, sitting in a chair, began to eat. The prince was appalled. "You have lied to me!" he shouted. "You told me you were a chicken!" "But I am a chicken," said the old woman. "I can sit at a table and eat and still be a chicken." The prince thought about this for some time. Then he, too, crawled out from under the table and joined the old woman. They ate in silence for some time. Then the prince began to laugh. For all we know, he is laughing still.

The story has a very happy ending. The prince went on to become the greatest king the kingdom had ever known. Under his rule, freedom grew in the kingdom and each person became free to be the person that they were meant to be. The people who had once been productive and happy also became wise.[10]

This story can have many meanings. But on one level it is a story of friendship. The old woman became friends with the prince. She accepted him as he was and didn't try to tell him who he should be. She accepted him as a chicken and was then able

10. Remen, *My Grandfather's Blessings*, 283–86.

to lead him into freedom. Friends share a deep respect for the uniqueness of the other person and the belief in the importance of their friend to become the person that God meant them to be. The old woman had supported the integrity of the prince.

13. FRIENDS: HELP BUILD A SOCIETY WHERE IT IS EASIER FOR PEOPLE TO BE GOOD

One of the reasons Dorothy Day liked Peter Maurin was that Peter understood that when life is stripped down to its very essentials, it is surprising how simple things become. Fewer and fewer things really matter and those that do, matter a great deal more. One of Peter's goals in working with Dorothy and the Catholic Worker Movement was to build a society where it would be easier for people to be good and thereby be of service to each other.

Peter possessed an unshakable conviction that all of life itself was holy. This insight had sustained him and became one of the foundation stones that he and Dorothy lived by. He had discovered we live not by choice but by grace and that life itself in all its forms is a blessing.

People who have had a near death experience often have an additional insight. Their experience has revealed to them that every life serves a single purpose. We are here to grow in wisdom and to learn to love better. Despite the countless and diverse ways we live our lives, every life is a spiritual path, and all life has a spiritual agenda. Peter and Dorothy both believed that these ideas have the power to change the way we see ourselves and the world. Just like Peter and Dorothy, friends help each other to see the world in this way and encourage each other when life becomes difficult. They help each other to free the hidden holiness in everything and everyone.

Peter and Dorothy believed that we restore the holiness of the world through our loving kindness and compassion. Everyone participates. It is a collective task. Every act of loving kindness, no matter how great or small, repairs the world. When we are good to others, we bless them and we free the goodness in them and in ourselves.

They also believed that each person makes a difference and that together we can heal the world. They felt that together we could return to what is most genuine and real in each of us. However, there is much in life that distracts us from our true natures. Sometimes it's greed, money, power, or desire. But our friends are there to help each other stay the course and focus on what really matters. Friends call forth this kind of goodness in each other.

Maybe the greatest service that friends provide for each other is simply to find ways to strengthen and live closer to our goodness. However, this is far from easy. It requires an everyday attention, an awareness of all that diminishes us, distracts us, and causes us to forget who we truly are. Our friends are graces given to us to help us with this endeavor.

14. THE AGING OF FRIENDSHIPS AND FRIENDSHIPS OF THE AGING

Famous Swiss psychiatrist Carl Jung believed that "every midlife crisis is a spiritual crisis, that we are called to die to the old self (ego), the fruit of the first half of life and liberate the new man or woman within us." He said,

> Wholly unprepared, they embark upon the second half of life. Or are there perhaps colleges for forty-year-olds which prepare them for their coming life and its demands as the ordinary colleges introduce our young people to a knowledge of the world and of life? No, there are none. Thoroughly unprepared we take the step into the afternoon of life; worse still, we take this step with the false presupposition that our truths and ideas will serve as hitherto. But we cannot live the afternoon of life according to the programme of life's morning—for what was great in the morning will be little at evening,

and what in the morning was true will at evening have become a lie.[11]

Jung divided life into two phases. The first phase, or "morning," is reserved for relating and orienting to the outer world by developing the ego. The second half, or "afternoon," is for adapting to the inner world by developing the full and true self. The midlife transition between these two Jung likened to a difficult birth.

This transition can be difficult because it involves a real breakdown of our old spiritual and psychic structures—the old masks and personas that have served us well in the past but no longer fit. The overarching roles that created the theme song for our lives begin to lose their music. It's anguish to come to that place in life where you know all the words but none of the music.

In our youth, we set up inner myths and stories to live by, but around the midlife juncture these patterns begin to crumble. It feels to us like a collapsing of all that is, but it's a holy quaking. "When order crumbles" writes John Shea, "mystery rises."[12]

One of my favorite Scripture passages comes from Ecclesiastes: "To everything there is a season, and a time for every purpose under heaven: a time to be born, and a time to die; a time to plant, and a time to pluck up that which is planted" (Eccl 3:1–2). We need reassurance that it's okay to let the old masks die, to "pluck up" what was planted long ago.

A friend said to me a long time ago, "if you think God leads you only beside still waters, think again. God will also lead you beside turbulent waters. If you have the courage to enter, you'll think you're drowning. But actually you're being churned into something new. It's ok, dive in."

Jung also believed that we all have a "shadow"; it's the rejected, inferior person inside we have always ignored and fought becoming. But when this fullness of time comes to each of us, a sacred voice at the heart of us cries out, shaking the old foundation. It draws us into a turbulence that forces us to confront our

---

11. Jung, "Stages of Life," 783.
12. Shea, *Stories of God*, 29.

deepest issues. It's as if some inner, divine grace seeks our growth and becoming and will plunge us, if need be, into a cauldron that seethes with questions and voices we would just as soon not hear. One way or another, the false roles, identities, and illusions spill over the sides of our life, and we are forced to stand in the chaos.

Without such upheaval, we would likely go on as always. It's so like us to deny things until some jolting moment—something we call an "eye-opening" experience—comes along and sharpens our vision.

"There is a self within each one of us aching to be born," says theologian Alan Jones.[13] And when this aching breaks into our lives—whether through a midlife struggle or some other crisis—we must somehow find the courage to say yes. Yes to this more real, more Christ-like self struggling to be born.

Traveling through these transitions is like coming out of a storm into calmer waters. And as we allow this more Christ-like self to be born in us, there are many personal and relational implications. Personally, we feel more real, more integrated, more unified. We feel like our true selves are finally emerging. There is no longer a need to wear our masks that got us through the first half of life. And because we feel more personally authentic, we know these changes in ourselves can have tremendous implications for our relationships. Just like with ourselves, we can be more genuine and authentic with our friends. With them too, we no longer need to wear any masks and we can "let them in," so to speak, to see "the real me." This freedom to be our true self allows our friendships to mature and deepen. This is one of the reasons why, as we grow older and mature, some people feel a new birth within themselves that not only enhances their own personal lives but opens up many opportunities for friendships. Reflecting on the later stages of life, the poet Robert Browning wrote, "Come grow old with me, the best is yet to be."

Through the years, as our lives entwine themselves with others, we realize how fortunate we have been to have been blessed with our friendships. Some of these have thrived for many years.

13. Jones, *Journey into Christ*, 52.

And as the twilight settles over our lives, we understand what wonderful graces our friends have been to us. We realize that friends on our spiritual journey are envoys of the overflowing grace an attentive God lavishes on us. With C. S. Lewis, we can say "You have not chosen one another but I have chosen you for one another."[14]

Aristotle said that good persons make the best friends, because in each there is so much that is worthy of love. Whether in times of good fortune or in times of adversity, friends will seek out one another because they are prepared to share sorrows as well as joys. It is truly a wonderful grace to have cultivated friendships that have endured through the years, because these are the people with whom we can share both our sorrows and our joys. These are the friends who, over the years, get to know us very well. There is a certain familiarity with them and a trust that allows us to believe that they will always be there for us. Even at a distance, which was so true for Therese of Lisieux and Maurice Belliere as well as Elizabeth Ann Seton and the Filicchi family, we know that these friends accept us for who we are and only want what is best for us. And as we age, we realize more and more that these friends are special gifts given to us on our journey through life.

As friendships age, there is both joy and sorrow. Joy because we realize what a gift our friends have been to us for so many years and gratitude for the grace of their presence. With them, our journey has been so much more meaningful. And as we reflect on our own aging, our hearts are filled with gratitude to God because their lives have been entwined with ours.

But there is also sorrow. Maybe it's the sorrow because we or our friends become sick. Or, perhaps our sorrow stems from the reality that more of our friends begin to die. But perhaps even these realities can serve the purpose of not taking our friends for granted. Realizing all of this can encourage us to keep in touch with our friends.

Yet, besides joy and sorrow there is also a letting go that is required as we age. It requires a surrender that can be very difficult. Sometimes, it is a letting go of our ability to see our friends

14. Lewis, *The Four Loves*, 126.

as much as we would like to because either circumstances in their lives or in ours change. For, example, if we see a friend deteriorating physically or mentally, it might require them to move, which would limit our ability to see them. They might move away, perhaps nearer to a family member who can help take care of them. Or, if they have dementia, they might need to move to a facility where they can receive the care that they need. This kind of letting go can certainly be challenging and difficult to cope with.

However, another challenge as we age, is to be open to cultivating new friends. As we said before, we never know when and in what circumstances a new friend might come into our lives. Sometimes, as we grow older, we can tend to close in on ourselves and close off opportunities for cultivating new friends. If we do this, then we are actually limiting the grace of the Lord as we grow older. Moreover, if we are able to cultivate new friends as we age, it brings a certain peace, contentment, and happiness to our later years.

15. FRIENDS: PAINFUL PARTINGS: WHEN FRIENDS WALK AWAY

St. Aelred of Rievaulx encouraged people to choose their friends carefully because this person was to be a partner in the love of God—a kindred spirit. St. Francis de Sales believed friends were gifts given to each other along the way—bright mirrors of the steadfast, overflowing reality of God's eternal love. Perhaps this is why it is so painful when friendships don't work out. Maybe this is what my professor meant so many years ago when he said "if you have a relationship that is bad, there is hardly anything worse."

Everyone has experienced broken friendships or friendships that haven't endured. No doubt each person has his or her own understanding of what went wrong to cause the friendship to deteriorate. Nevertheless, the pain endures—sometimes for a long time. These "painful partings" can happen in a variety of ways.

When Friends Walk Away

Even Jesus experienced the painful reality of people walking away from him and wondered if his apostles would also walk away. In chapter six of John's Gospel, Jesus is explaining how he will give himself to people as his own flesh and blood. But many of them could not accept this teaching. "This is intolerable language," they said. "How could anyone accept it?" Then John continues, "After this, many of his disciples left Him and stopped going with Him." Jesus even wondered if his closest friends would walk away. On a human level, how hurt and disappointed he must have been. He turned to the Twelve and asked, "What about you, do you also want to walk away?" Simon Peter answered, "Lord, who shall we go to? You have the words of eternal life" (John 6:60–69).

When we lose a friend, for whatever reason, it is always painful. If we lose a friend because of sickness or death or perhaps because a friend moves away, there is always a profound sense of loss. This was so true for Therese of Lisieux and Maurice Belliere as well as Elizabeth Ann Seton and the Filicchi family. However, when a friend walks away for no apparent reason or for a reason we don't understand, there is also an emotional wrenching that takes place that deepens the feeling of loss. This happened to me years ago when I was in my twenties and it is still extremely vivid to me. I had a good friend for over three years but it was a long-distance friendship because we lived in different states and it was before computers, mobile devices, Facebook, Skype, etc. We rarely got to see each other but we wrote cards and letters, spoke on the phone, and made tapes for each other. These were our ways of cultivating the friendship. For me, this person was certainly a "kindred spirit," a gift given to me along my journey, a "bright mirror of God's steadfast eternal love." And I thought it was the same for her. For over three years this friendship was a great blessing to me in life. Aristotle connects friendship and happiness and I could truly say this relationship brought me much happiness. It also gave me a lot of energy and zest for life. Then, gradually, things began to change. The cards, letters and phone calls came less frequently.

As I began to realize all of this, I would try to talk with her about these changes and how she saw the relationship changing, but to no avail. For some reason, she would not answer. Interiorly, I began to panic. I felt lost, abandoned, angry, and sad. As I desperately searched for answers, I became more and more depressed. Over a period of several more weeks, the friendship ended. It took me many months to begin to work my way out of this depression. Clearly for me, this was a "painful parting."

Sometimes friends walk away because they disagree with a decision we made. Over twenty-five years ago, after much prayer and reflection, I made a decision that my friend, Sam, disagreed with. He thought it was too extreme. In the beginning, he seemed fine with it. But over the ensuing months, I began to hear from him less frequently. One day I called to invite him and his wife to our home for dinner. It was then that he told me directly that he didn't want to see me anymore. At first, I was shocked. Sam never seemed like the type of person that would end a good friendship because of one decision. Life is full of difficult decisions that are immensely painful to make. I never thought that my decision would impact our friendship in this way. One would hope our good friends would support us in these decisions.

But this story doesn't end here. One day, about four years ago, I was at home reading and the phone rang. Who do you suspect was on the other end? Yes, it was Sam. After all these years, he had called to apologize and ask my forgiveness for the way he had treated me. He wanted to get together to talk. So, we arranged a time for me to go to his home and he explained why he had ended our friendship. Over the years Sam had survived cancer, left the Catholic Church, and joined a Protestant church, which he felt was very life-giving. In the process, he felt compelled to review his life and try to heal any broken relationships. For me, this was truly a redemptive moment. Over the last several years, we have reconnected and become friends once again. I consider it one of the major graces of my life.

Sometimes, groups walk away. Dan had been a friend for over twenty years. One day he told me about an experience of friendship that had been extremely painful for him. This time the pain involved a group of friends. Dan had been a member of a religious community for many years. During this time, he had formed many friendships with members of his community. Certainly, in one sense, he felt they were all his brothers. With time, several became good friends who shared life deeply. After approximately fifteen years, Dan said he began to become very depressed. He decided to go to counseling to help sort out the issues that were facing him. After much prayer and soul searching, Dan decided to leave the community. It was the most difficult decision he ever had to make in his life. He said he realized his decision would change the nature of his friendships with his brothers. He just didn't realize how much. Dan said he planned to stay in touch with his good friends in the community, but soon realized they didn't want that. After several attempts were made to continue his friendships, it gradually became clear that his efforts were not reciprocal. Even his best friend, he said, didn't want to stay in touch. He said he had struggled so much just to make this decision and felt devastated when his friends in the community didn't want to remain friends.

But this story also has a redemptive moment. He went on to tell me that years after he had left the community, his best friend in the community called him one day unexpectedly and wanted to come and see him. Of course, Dan wanted this too. So his friend came to his home and apologized for the way he had treated him over the years. Although the friendship did not return to the way it was in the community, Dan nevertheless felt this was a great grace for him in his life. It was clearly a healing moment.

On the other hand, sometimes groups and organizations can become our friends. This became very clear to me after our first child, a son, was stillborn. His death was such a painful parting that caused a tremendous sadness for my wife and me. It's the kind of loss that I believe you don't ever really get over. You just try to grieve, to cope as best you can and continue on. Before we left the hospital that day, over twenty-eight years ago, we were put in touch with the group Compassionate Friends. It is a support group for people who have lost loved ones. My wife and I went to several meetings and these people were extremely helpful to us. We have always been very grateful to them. As a result of this experience, grief therapy became a specialty area for me as a therapist. Moreover, through the years, I have given numerous talks to this group as a way of saying "thank you." Over the years, this group of people has become true friends of mine.

When friendships end, for whatever reason, it is certainly one of the most painful realities of human relationships. The loss we feel can be very intense. But how we deal with this loss can make all the difference.

We cannot protect ourselves from loss. Yet, many people try to employ strategies that shelter themselves from feeling loss. But if we do this, we cannot use the experience to grow, because none of them lead to healing. Although denial, rationalization, substitution, and avoidance may numb the pain of broken friendships, every one of them hurts us in some far more fundamental ways. None is respectful toward life or toward process. None acknowledges our capacity for finding meaning or wisdom. Pain often marks the place where self-knowledge and growth can happen, much in the same way fear does.

Grieving is the way loss can heal. Yet many people do not know how to grieve and heal from their losses. This makes it difficult to participate fully in life. At some deep level, it may make us unwilling to be open to others or afraid of becoming attached or intimate with another human being. It may keep us from reaching out and making friends in the future. Many people have become *emotional couch potatoes* because they do not know how to heal their hearts.

Unless we learn to grieve, we may need to live life at a distance in order to protect ourselves from pain. We may not be able to risk having anything that really matters to us or allow ourselves to be touched, to be intimate, to care or be cared about. Untouched, we will suffer, and we will not be transformed by our suffering. Grieving may be one of the most fundamental life skills. It is the way the heart can heal from loss and go on to love again and grow wise.

Conclusion

Last year, as I turned seventy, my wife wanted to have a big party for me. I was not so sure that I wanted to celebrate this milestone in this way. But as we talked more about it, I began to think this kind of celebration would be good because it would give me the opportunity to thank these friends for their presence in my life. It would allow me to share with them what tremendous graces they had been to me through the years. As it turned out, I was glad we had the party.

There is a line in a favorite song of mine that says, "we come from a long line of love." And this is so true in the rich tradition of our Catholic faith. We come from a long line of believers—people like you and me—who strove for holiness in their lives like we do in ours. But sometimes we have the tendency to think about those in our past tradition—especially the saints—as *always* being *St.* Teresa or *St.* Elizabeth Ann Seton. It's almost as if we have made them saints from the beginning of their lives. It is easy to forget they were people just like us with all the same struggles, temptations, joys, and sorrows of life that we experience. They too, like us, continually tried to love God and others more and more. It's so important to remember that they *became* saints. They were not *born* saints. And, in the course of their journeys, other people became very important to them. Their friends helped them become the person God wanted them to be.

We, too, on our journeys, are striving to love God and others as best we can. We too, are striving to grow in holiness—to become saints. Each person is unique and original just like the saints and each one of us have been given certain people on our journeys to help us in a variety of ways. No one has lived what we have lived. We have to trust that our stories too, deserve to be told. Our stories need to be shared because the people we have met on our journeys are graces given to us to encourage, and they inspire us to become saints. We may even discover that the better we tell our stories, the better we will want to live them.

This book is meant to be both encouraging and inspirational. Understanding the importance of friendship from several Christian and non-Christian writers and drawing on the stories of several saints and holy people, we have seen how important their friends were to them—special graces on their journeys. At the same time, we have listened to the stories of other "ordinary" people that can also be encouraging and inspirational in our own efforts at striving for holiness. These stories of "ordinary people" help us understand the *grace of friendship* in our own lives. Hopefully, these stories will lead us closer to the One who has called each of us his friend.

Bibliography

Aelred of Rievaulx. *Spiritual Friendship*. Kalamazoo, MI: Cistercian, 1977.

Ahern, Patrick. *Maurice and Therese: The Story of a Love*. New York: Doubleday, 1998.

———, speaker. *St. Therese: The Saint for Me*. Audiocassette. West Covina, CA: St. Joseph Communications, 1997.

Albom, Mitch. *Tuesdays with Morrie*. New York: Doubleday, 1997.

Aristotle. *Ethica Nichomachea*. Translated by W. D. Ross. New York: Random House, 1941.

Aschenbrenner, George. "A Hidden Self Grown Strong." In *Handbook of Spirituality for Ministers*, edited by Robert J. Wicks, 228–48. New York: Paulist, 1995.

Au, Wilkie. *By Way of the Heart: Toward a Holistic Christian Spirituality*. New York: Paulist, 1989.

Barry, William. *God's Passionate Desire and Our Response*. Notre Dame, IN: Ave Maria, 1993.

Clark, Elizabeth. *Jerome, Chrysostom and Friends*. New York: Mellen, 1979.

Coles, Robert. *Dorothy Day: A Radical Devotion*. Reading, MA: Perseus, 1987.

———. "Moral Leadership: Dorothy Day and Peter Maurin." *America*, June 6, 1998, 5–14.

Crossin, James. *Friendship: The Key to Spiritual Growth*. New York: Paulist, 1987.

Cunningham, Larry, and Keith Egan. *Christian Spirituality*. New York: Paulist, 1996.

Dailey, Thomas. *Praying with Francis de Sales*. Winona, MN: St. Mary's, 1997.

Day, Dorothy. *Loaves and Fishes*. Maryknoll, NY: Orbis, 1997.

———. *The Long Loneliness*. San Francisco: HarperCollins, 1952.

de Mello, Anthony. *The Heart of the Enlightened*. New York: Doubleday, 1989.

de Sales, Francis. *Introduction to a Devout Life*. New York: Doubleday, 1989.

Dirvin, Joseph. *Mrs. Seton*. New York: Basilica of the National Shrine of St. Elizabeth Ann Seton, 1993.

Downey, Michael. *Understanding Christian Spirituality*. New York: Paulist, 1997.

Dreyer, Elizabeth. *Earth Crammed with Heaven: A Spirituality of Everyday Life.* New York: Paulist, 1994.

Dubay, Thomas. *Fire Within.* San Francisco: Ignatius, 1989.

Dulles, Avery. "Orthodoxy and Social Change." *America* 51 (1998) 8–17.

Fremantle, W. H. "The Principle Works of St. Jerome." In vol. 6 of *A Select Library of Nicene and Post Nicene Fathers of the Christian Church.* Grand Rapids: Eerdmans, 1989.

Fromm, Erich. *The Art of Loving.* New York: Harper & Row, 1956.

Fulghum, Robert. *It Was on Fire When I Lay Down on It.* New York: Ballantine, 1988.

Givey, David. *The Social Thought of Thomas Merton.* Cincinnati: Franciscan, 1984.

Grant, Michael. *Cicero: On the Good Life.* New York: Penguin, 1984.

Houselander, Caryll. *The Risen Christ.* New York: Sheed & Ward, 1958.

————. *A Rocking Horse Catholic.* New York: Sheed & Ward, 1955.

Hughes, Alfred. *Spiritual Masters.* Huntington, IN: Our Sunday Visitor, 1988.

Jerome, Saint. *The Letters of St. Jerome.* Vol. 1. Translated by Charles Mierow. New York: Newman, 1963.

————. *Select Letters of St. Jerome.* Translated by F. A. Wright. Cambridge: Harvard University Press, 1933.

Jones, Alan. *Exploring Spiritual Direction.* New York: Seabury, 1982.

————. *Journey into Christ.* San Francisco: Harper & Row, 1977.

Jung, C. *The Structure and Dynamics of the Psyche.* Collected Works of C. G. Jung 8. Translated by R. F. C. Hull. New Jersey: Princeton University Press, 1960.

Kavanaugh, K., and O. Rodriguez. *The Collected Works of St. Teresa of Avila.* Washington, DC: ICS, 1987.

Kelly, J. N. D. *Jerome: His Life, Writings and Controversies.* Peabody, MA: Hendrickson, 1998.

Kushner, Harold. *How Good Do We Have to Be?* Boston: Little, Brown, & Company: 1996.

Leclercq, Jean. *The Love of Learning and the Desire for God.* New York: Fordham, 1961.

Lewis, C. S. *The Four Loves.* New York: Harcourt, 1960.

Marie Celeste, Sister, S. C. *The Intimate Friendships of Elizabeth Ann Bailey Seton.* New York: Paulist, 1989.

May, Gerald. *The Awakened Heart.* New York: HarperCollins, 1991.

McGinn, Bernard. *The Doctors of the Church.* New York: Crossroad, 1999.

Merton, Thomas. *Conjectures of a Guilty Bystander.* New York: Image, 1968.

————. *Disputed Questions.* New York: Farrar, Straus & Giroux, 1953.

————. *Love and Living.* New York: Bantam, 1980.

————. *The New Man.* New York: Farrar, Straus & Giroux, 1961.

————. *New Seeds of Contemplation.* New York: New Directions, 1961.

Monceaux, Paul. *St. Jerome: The Early Years.* London: Sheed & Ward, 1933.

Nouwen, Henri. *Pray to Live.* New York: Fides, 1972.

O'Donohue, James. *Anam Cara*. San Francisco: HarperCollins, 1997.

Peck, Scott. *The Different Drum*. New York: Simon & Schuster, 1987.

—. *A World Waiting to Be Born*. New York: Bantam, 1993.

Ramsey, Boniface. *John Cassian: The Conferences*. New York: Paulist, 1997.

Rees, E. "A Woman in Love with God." *Catholic Digest*, April 1994, 57–61.

Remen, Rachel. *My Grandfather's Blessings*. New York: Riverhead, 2000.

Rilke, Rainer Maria. *Letters to a Young Poet*. New York: Norton, 1934.

Rolheiser, Ronald. *The Holy Longing*. New York: Doubleday, 1999.

Second Vatican Council. *Dogmatic Constitution on the Church: Lumen Gentium*. Boston: St. Paul, 1964.

Sellner, Edward. "An Inclination of the Heart." *Spiritual Life* (Fall 2001) 161–77.

Shannon, William. *Silent Lamp*. New York: Crossroads, 1994.

Shea, John. *Stories of God: An Unauthorized Biography*. Chicago: Thomas More, 1978.

Steinmann, Jean. *Saint Jerome and His Times*. Notre Dame: Fides, 1959.

Teresa of Avila. *The Way of Perfection*. Westminster, MD: Newman, 1961.

Therese of Lisieux. *The Story of a Soul*. New York: Doubleday, 1989.

Wadell, Paul. *Friendship and the Moral Life*. Notre Dame: University of Notre Dame Press, 1989.

Ward, Maisie. *Caryll Houselander: That Divine Eccentric*. New York: Sheed & Ward, 1962.

White, Caroline. *Christian Friendship in the Fourth Century*. New York: Cambridge University Press, 1992.

—. *The Correspondence (394–419) Between Jerome and Augustine of Hippo*. Lewiston, NY: Mellen, 1990.

Wicks, M. "Teresa of Jesus: Model and Mentor for Ministry." In *Handbook of Spirituality*, edited by Robert Wicks, 115–28. New York: Paulist, 1995.

Wright, Wendy. *Bond of Perfection*. New York: Paulist, 1985.

—. "Reflections on Spiritual Friendship Between Men and Women." *Weavings*, July–August, 1987, 22–34.

—. *A Retreat with Francis de Sales, Jane de Chantal and Aelred of Rievaulx*. Cincinnati: St. Anthony Messenger, 1996.